ΠF173451

Palgrave Studies in Austrian Economics

Series Editors

David Howden
Madrid Campus
Saint Louis University
Madrid, Spain

Philipp Bagus
Economia Aplicada I
Universidad Rey Juan Carlos
Madrid, Spain

This series provides insights to the key debates within Austrian economics. It presents advanced research that links current discussions on Austrian economics within its rich and influential intellectual tradition. Bringing together books from the leading researchers in this field, the varied the series aims to define the current scope of research within Austrian economics and shape directions of future analysis, with entries that offer both a foundation to the topic for those new to Austrian economics and fresh insights and debates for those who are well versed on the topic.

Antony P. Mueller

A Primer on Austrian Macroeconomics

Austrian Capital Theory for Macroeconomic
Research and Teaching

Antony P. Mueller
Mises Academy
São Paulo, Brazil

ISSN 3005-0464 ISSN 3005-0472 (electronic)
Palgrave Studies in Austrian Economics
ISBN 978-3-031-75188-2 ISBN 978-3-031-75189-9 (eBook)
https://doi.org/10.1007/978-3-031-75189-9

© The Editor(s) (if applicable) and The Author(s), under exclusive license to Springer Nature Switzerland AG 2024

This work is subject to copyright. All rights are solely and exclusively licensed by the Publisher, whether the whole or part of the material is concerned, specifically the rights of translation, reprinting, reuse of illustrations, recitation, broadcasting, reproduction on microfilms or in any other physical way, and transmission or information storage and retrieval, electronic adaptation, computer software, or by similar or dissimilar methodology now known or hereafter developed.
The use of general descriptive names, registered names, trademarks, service marks, etc. in this publication does not imply, even in the absence of a specific statement, that such names are exempt from the relevant protective laws and regulations and therefore free for general use.
The publisher, the authors and the editors are safe to assume that the advice and information in this book are believed to be true and accurate at the date of publication. Neither the publisher nor the authors or the editors give a warranty, expressed or implied, with respect to the material contained herein or for any errors or omissions that may have been made. The publisher remains neutral with regard to jurisdictional claims in published maps and institutional affiliations.

This Palgrave Macmillan imprint is published by the registered company Springer Nature Switzerland AG.
The registered company address is: Gewerbestrasse 11, 6330 Cham, Switzerland

If disposing of this product, please recycle the paper.

Contents

CHAPTER 1

Introduction

Abstract Since the 1970s, Austrian economics has experienced a renaissance. The Austrian approach gains relevance due to its internal consistency and the ability to explain many phenomena outside the scope of conventional economics. Austrian macroeconomics provides a paradigm capable of effectively addressing policy issues related to the business cycle, inflation, employment, and economic growth and development.

Keywords Austrian economics • Business cycle • Stagflation • Economic policy • Consistent paradigm

Almost silenced during the rule of Keynesian Economics during the 1950s and 1960s, Austrian economics experienced a comeback in the 1970s. One cause behind the renaissance of Austrian economics was the helplessness of Keynesian demand-side policies in the face of stagflation. The other reason was that Friedrich August von Hayek received the Nobel Prize in Economic Science in 1974. In the 1980s, monetarism and supply-side economics incorporated various aspects of Austrian economics into their policy suggestions, and in the 1990s, the institutionalization of Austrian economics advanced with the establishment of the Ludwig von Mises Institute in the United States, which has been imitated around the world ever since.

© The Author(s), under exclusive license to Springer Nature
Switzerland AG 2024
A. P. Mueller, *A Primer on Austrian Macroeconomics*,
Palgrave Studies in Austrian Economics,
https://doi.org/10.1007/978-3-031-75189-9_1

Today, Austrian economics is a rapidly growing school of economics. Many of the fundamental features of Austrian economics remain still largely unknown to the students and professors of economics. The macroeconomic part of the Austrian School receives even less attention at most universities. Yet this may be ending because one of the major contributions of Austrian macroeconomics is its business cycle theory. There have been little advances in mainstream macroeconomics since the rise of the rational expectations theory, which, curiously enough, already contained elements of the Austrian approach. The full relevance of Austrian economics still needs to be discovered. After all, Austrian macroeconomics distinguishes itself by having a fully developed business cycle theory and a body of knowledge that is both flexible and internally consistent.

It is not only economic crises that continue to happen which expose the intellectual deficiencies of the mainstream. Additionally, the failure of current monetary policy, which is guided by the inflation-targeting concept and the "Dynamic Stochastic General Equilibrium" (DSGE) model shows up in the return of price inflation in the United States and in Europe. It is no surprise that conventional theory has little to offer to explain the recurrences of economic and financial crises and is largely clueless when it comes to macroeconomic policy. There are many models, but little consistency. There is much formalism, but little substance. Economic policy is ruled by the application of simplistic rules while a large part of modern economics research is practically irrelevant. All in all, modern macroeconomics as it is represented in the popular textbooks and in the curricula of university economics has become a dull discipline which is abandoned by students, fallen in esteem by the press, and largely ignored by the public. The effect of the drastic fall in enrollment in the study of economics shows up in the decline of the quality of the public discussion of economic and social matters.

Yet there is hope. Many young people who discover Austrian Economics embrace its approach with enthusiasm. They are likewise attracted to the intellectual quality of Austrian economics as to its usefulness as a tool for understanding many aspects of social life. Different from mainstream economics, the Austrian school does not favor formalism but substance and its suggestions for macroeconomics are stunning. Austrian economics excels by its consistency and its ability to handle complexity. It is no surprise that Austrian economics has become the most vibrant school of economics that is currently in existence.

Mainstream economists can no longer afford to ignore Austrian economics. The demand among students to learn sound economics is rising. The public craves for solid economics as people are tired of being fed with the superficialities and distortions that they hear from politicians and their minions who act as self-declared experts. People have lost trust in the mass media and have become frustrated by the inconsistencies of the kind of economics that are presented to the public. When the time for an idea has come, nothing can stop it and this is now the case with Austrian economics.

Austrian macroeconomics rejects the belief of modern macroeconomics that when an economy achieves the desired rates of economic growth along with the established inflation target, monetary policy would be at an optimal stance. It is shown how central bank authorities tend to be misled by their data analysis of the price level, of economic growth, and of employment and why active central banking inadvertently will initiate boom-bust cycles by fostering the emergence of unsustainable production structures. Without central bank interference, productivity increases would bring about temporary deflation and, left to its natural path, rising profits and a higher purchasing power would move the economy toward an expansion and increased expenditures without recession. However, with central bank interventions which are directed at maintaining the so-called price level stability as defined by the inflation target, monetary authorities will expand the money supply and transform a productivity-led wealth increase into a debt-driven excessive boom, which produces the foundation for the bust later and will push the economy into depression.

At the theoretical level, this book provides a contribution to the integration of capital theory into monetary and macro theory. It is shown how business cycles emerge and develop and how misleading interest signals as the result of central bank policies bring about unsustainable production structures. This approach allows for bridging the gap between micro- and macroeconomics and between the short-run and the long-run analysis.

At the policy level, the approach presented here leads to the conclusion that not much different from aggregate demand management, inflation targeting, too, does not guarantee stable economic growth but is prone to produce booms that can easily get out of hand and consequently turn into busts because they cannot be diagnosed as such within the analytic framework of both labor- and money-based macroeconomics due to the nonattendance to the role of capital and the structure of production.

In periods of lesser productivity gains, the inflationary bias of modern central banks produces stagflation, as expansive monetary policy feeds directly into higher consumer prices. It is mainly under the conditions of high productivity gains or when other factors bring down production costs on a large scale that central banks have an easy shot to achieve "price-level stability" and hold the inflation rate within the established target for some time. The critical stage and the turning point will take place when the phase of concentrated technological progress ends or when an adverse supply shock occurs. Then, the foundation on which the pyramid of debt was erected breaks away. Debt-free growth could have been achieved if the central bank had let the deflationary episode work itself out. Instead, the monetary authorities, in their fixation to avoid deflation at all costs, have created a credit-driven boom. At the first stage of the monetary expansion, the artificially depressed interest rate produces an economic upswing; at the peak of the boom, the debt load has made the economy ever more vulnerable to adverse shocks. Shocks that would hardly affect a robust economy then represent a threat. Central bank management becomes increasingly precarious, and the tendency grows to fight as long as possible against any potential downturn with further increases in the money supply.

Because of the monetary expansion, it appears as if more savings seems were present than there are de facto in terms of the availability of resources. Thus, the demand for investment goods, particularly at the early stages of the production process, will increase along with the demand for consumer goods. At the end of the boom phase, productivity gains peter out or adverse supply side shocks occur that no longer can be easily absorbed. With the absence of compensating productivity gains, monetary pumping now feeds directly into goods prices. If central banks continue with monetary expansion, more price inflation will result. With prices rising, the monetary multiplier and the velocity of circulation tend to increase and drive up the price level even faster. If, however, central banks try to counter the higher price level with a restrictive monetary policy, they typically lose control of the monetary multiplier and the contraction of the velocity of circulation will amplify the restrictive stance of monetary policy. The excessive boom is followed by an excessive contraction.

Strong economic booms are characterized by high productivity gains due to new technology and often by a concurrent increase in the supply of cheap labor. By not allowing deflation to run its course under these conditions, central banks boost the boom while they formally meet their low inflation target. They provide ample liquidity in a situation when a falling price level is required. The expansion of the money supply beyond authentic savings comes along with increasing debt levels. In such a situation, fabricated by ingenious central banks, when an excessive debt level relative to the productive base has been reached, deflation indeed becomes a problem. In a low-debt economy, the positive effects of deflation in terms of increased purchasing power outweigh its negative side and are beneficial. In a high-debt economy, deflation becomes a vicious factor. Therefore, modern central banks will try to make the debt surge go on as far and as long as they can. As long as the institutional setting of modern central banks continues to exist in its present form, they will fight deflation even when it is beneficial. The monetary authorities will rather feed the boom as long as the inflation rate remains moderate. This way, they prepare the path for a vicious deflation to happen in the bust phase of the business cycle.

By expanding the money supply and thereby bringing the monetary interest rate down, central banks transform the productivity-led economic expansion into a debt-driven boom. At the upper turning point of the cycle, the liquidity, which has been accumulated by various rounds of monetary expansion that were initiated to fight deflationary tendencies, shows up as open inflation when the productivity gains peter out or when negative supply side shocks occur. It is at this stage, when monetary policy loses control, as its instruments cannot be adequately calibrated in the inflationary phase and later in the contractive phase.

Austrian economics is consistently opposed to interventionism in the markets—because of both theoretical reasons and empirical evidence. Interventionism does not work as conceived by the planner. The belief is still widespread that a so-called third way would be needed, a system that would combine "the best of" capitalism and socialism. In this view, the ideal socioeconomic system would be one where capitalism is tamed like a wild beast and where this animal is kept under the authority of the state. Yet the adherents of this model forget that politicians are self-interested and people are deceivable. It does not take much fantasy to see that once interventionism is taken for granted as the right political system, there won't be an end to interventionist activity until the economy is fully destroyed. Yet the demands of social justice and social security are unlimited. Destroying entrepreneurial capitalism in favor of state capitalism and socialism leads to economic decline.

The need is widely felt, even among mainstream economists, that the currently dominant paradigm is deficient. By focusing on the short term, economics automatically becomes the maid of special interests—be it government, trade unions, political parties, or ideologies that are fashionable.

Some tendencies in microeconomics are also disturbing with its interventionist bias because of perceived "market failure" and the ongoing outreach of economic analysis into almost all areas of social life. This "imperialism of economics" seems to involve that, step after step, the premise of subjective valuation gets lost in favor of an authoritarian position.

The book is divided into four parts. The first part provides a prolegomenon to the study of Austrian macroeconomics and elucidates its basic principles. The second part is dedicated to the analysis of money and monetary policy in the perspective of Austrian economics. The objective of this section is the integration of capital into macroeconomics. The third part analyzes the interrelationship between the real and monetary sides of the economy.

CHAPTER 2

What Makes Austrian Macroeconomics Unique?

Abstract The concept of "human action" is central to Austrian economics. From this follows an emphasis on the role of the entrepreneur as the agent to deal with uncertainty and contingency in the production process. Prices are the essential tool of economic calculation. Therefore, economic rationality requires private property and competitive markets. Long before it became a topic in conventional macroeconomics, Austrian economics already emphasized the need for a micro-foundation of macroeconomics. Due to its realist method of analyzing causal relationships, with human action at its center, Austrian macroeconomics has been able to avoid excessive abstractions, confusing formalization, and fictitious model-making. Its usefulness as a tool of analysis has been proven again and again, particularly in times of economic turmoil when conventional macroeconomics tends to fail.

Keywords History of Austrian Economics • Human action • Contingency • Property • Markets • Methodology

© The Author(s), under exclusive license to Springer Nature
Switzerland AG 2024
A. P. Mueller, *A Primer on Austrian Macroeconomics*,
Palgrave Studies in Austrian Economics,
https://doi.org/10.1007/978-3-031-75189-9_2

1   ORIGIN OF AUSTRIAN ECONOMICS

"Austrian economics" is the study of human action based on the principles of praxeology. The main methodological principles of praxeology are methodological individualism, subjectivism, and marginalism of valuation. The name "Austrian economics" is derived from the fact that the founding authors of this school came from Austria. Adherents of Austrian economics can also be found as practitioners in business and finance and in politics.

The origin of Austrian economics reaches back to the school of Salamanca in the seventeenth century and as such it is the oldest school of economics. It began much earlier than the classical school. In several aspects, the so-called classical school of economics constituted a regress of knowledge compared to the early Spanish and French economic theories.

The modern foundations of Austrian economics were laid by Carl Menger and Eugen von Böhm-Bawerk. Ludwig von Mises and Friedrich August von Hayek refined the approach. Murray N. Rothbard was the most prominent representative in the United States (Holcombe 1999).

The unifying principles of the Austrian school are subjectivism of valuation, the marginalist and sequential character of human valuation, thinking, and action. Methodological principles of the Austrian school include the special attention that is given to time and the limits of knowledge as well as the recognition that social phenomena are complex.

The Austrian school proper as a well-defined scientific school emerged with the publication of Carl Menger's *Principles of Economics* (1871).

In contrast to the empiricist approach of the so-called historical school, Carl Menger saw the proper foundation of economics not in the objective world outside of human acts and valuations, but in the individual acts themselves, in the subjective valuations of the individual, and in human action. With Carl Menger, Austrian economics gained its prime principles of individualism, subjectivism, and marginalism. In continuation of this approach, Eugen von Böhm-Bawerk (1884) developed a theory of capital based on subjectivism. He was the first to introduce the concept of time into capital theory and to explain the interest rate in terms of time preferences. By focusing on the intertemporal aspects of capital, Böhm-Bawerk provided the basis for the development of the Austrian theory of the business cycle. Ludwig von Mises and Friedrich von Hayek, by elaborating on Böhm-Bawerk's approach, formulated a theory of the business cycle, which points to credit expansion as the start of the cycle when the monetary expansion exceeds sustainable funding in terms of available real resources, particularly in the form of the factors of production, such as nature (energy), capital, labor, and technology. Austrian macroeconomics interprets economic crises as a process of retrenchment, when the overexposure to capital formation gets corrected. In the perspective of Austrian macroeconomics, the Great Depression of the 1930s was the result of the policy of monetary overexpansion. This monetary excess did not show up immediately as price inflation because of the high productivity growth during the 1920s.

In the face of the Russian Revolution in 1917 and the establishment of a socialist economy after the consolidation of the Communist rule in Russia, Ludwig Mises and Friedrich Hayek became the leading exponents of the socialist calculation debate. Applying the principles of Austrian economics, Mises put forth the thesis of the "impossibility of rational calculation in socialism". In his *Calculation in the Socialist Commonwealth*, he stressed the problems of economic calculation in the absence of markets and property, while Friedrich Hayek elaborated his theories of knowledge and market coordination. Murray Rothbard systematized large parts of the Misesian theory. Besides becoming the leading figure of the libertarian movement, Rothbard's main contribution to general Austrian economic theory is his *Man, Economy, and the State* (1963), and in Austrian macroeconomics his analysis of "America's Great Depression" (1964) and his writing of money and monetary policy.

Austrian macroeconomics deals with the same problems as conventional macroeconomics but uses a different approach. Macroeconomic problems comprise issues such as employment and the price level, economic growth and development, and the issues of public finance.

2   Human Action

The prominent feature of Austrian economics is its individualistic-subjective approach to phenomena of human action. Economics represents a subcategory, albeit the most advanced, of the study of human action. While Austrian economics shares many elements with neoclassical economics, there are also several distinctive aspects, which make the Austrian approach unique and distinct from the mainstream.

Different from the approaches that dominate large parts of modern economics, Austrian economics is based on the concept of human action. As Ludwig von Mises declared in his Notes and Recollections, "what distinguishes the Austrian School and will lend it everlasting fame is its doctrine of economic action, in contrast to one of economic equilibrium or nonaction."

Mises called his approach "praxeology". Praxeology puts economics on a new footing with its basis in the principles of human action. As such, Austrian economics confronts human action in its full complexity. This research program aims nothing less than to create a general theory of society based on the principles of human action.

Human action is different from behavior. Behavior is a deterministic or probabilistic term. It leaves no room for proper human decision-making. In the context of the model of the homo economicus, the rationality of the logic of choice is contained in the premises of the setting. Modern microeconomics reduces rationality to logical deduction, and when de facto human behavior deviates from this postulate, irrationality of the agents is being claimed (which automatically calls for the intervention of the authorities to "correct" this "false" behavior).

It is different from human action. It is freedom of choice regarding purposes and means that distinguishes man from nature and the animal kingdom. The pursuit of purposes through systematic application of means is the basic characteristic of human existence.

All our main categories of thinking are contained in human action. It is with the axiom of human action that concepts are given such as purpose and means, profit and loss, pleasure and pain, time and sequence, past and present.

Instead of striving toward ever more reductionism and extreme simplifications, as it is characteristic of modern social sciences, Austrian economics takes up the challenge to deal with the complexity of economic reality and the contingency of human action.

The representatives of the so-called classical economics and its successors presumed that for economics to become "scientific" it must be as "deterministic" as a kind of social physics. In the meantime, however, modern natural science has largely abandoned the pure Newtonian paradigm. Nevertheless, the reductionist and deterministic focus still dominates large parts of the economics profession. One of the consequences of this kind of research is that its results are often useless and, worst of all, the recipes of this kind of deterministic economics are not only not adequate for our current problems but also often very harmful to their proper solution.

By being based on the principles of human action, Austrian economics is not only modern in the methodological sense, it is also modern in the choice of the objects of its research. Different from the schools of economics that study markets in a deterministic fashion with the aim to discover the features of a dead point called "equilibrium", Austrian economics studies markets as a process and does discard "optimizing behavior" in favor of purposeful human action.

In the view of Austrian economics, the essence of the economy is not given by aggregates that supposedly correlate with each other, but all economic phenomena are inherently those of human action. Long before it became seen as a necessity by other schools of economics, it has always been clear for Austrian economics that macroeconomics needs a micro-foundation.

Different from the behavioral approaches in the social sciences, the theory of human action is a doctrine of freedom of choice, individual endeavor, and personal responsibility.

The concept of human action contains its essential analytic concepts *a priori*. These include ends, ranking, sequence (time), and means as logical categories whose abstract validity is thought to be invariant and common to all men. They are essential to the definition of a human being as a purposeful (rational) and acting (active) being, and the meaning of these categories is directly given for the human mind.

> All the concepts and theorems of praxeology are implied in the category of human action. The first task is to extract and to deduce them, to expound their implications and to define the universal conditions of acting as such.

Rationality in the theory of human action is an analytic category; it is not a statement about actual behavior seen in the light of outside criteria. Values are subjective and variant, and they do not allow for inter-subjective comparisons. They also cannot be measured because measurement refers to outside phenomena. Praxeology studies human action and the logical implications of human actions from which it gains its central categories such as ends and means, valuation, time, data, scarcity, ranking, prices, money, and time.

Mises explains:

> What distinguishes the praxeological system from the logical system epistemologically is precisely that it implies the categories both of time and of causality. The praxeological system too is aprioristic and deductive. As a

system it is out of time. But change is one of its elements. The notions of sooner and later and of cause and effect are among its constituents. Anteriority and consequence are essential concepts of praxeological reasoning. So is the irreversibility of events. In the frame of the praxeological system any reference to functional correspondence is no less metaphorical and misleading than is the reference to anteriority and consequence in the frame of the logical system.

In the perspective of praxeology, human action is purposeful behavior. Individuals have aims that they try to obtain and for that purpose they apply means. Human action is means-ends oriented. It is active choice of both purpose and means with both examined by subjective valuation. In this sense, human action is tautological rational. This does not exclude that ends, as well as means, can be badly chosen and that means are wrong in the technical sense or purposes false by certain external standards.

Human thinking is interior human action. Both are imperfect and incomplete. Rather than the exception, shortcomings of thought and deed are essential to human condition. Indeed, these shortcomings of thought and deed represent the motor of social progress that moves humankind from one error to the next to eliminate one imperfection by another. While each person acts individually and subjectively rational, this does not mean that the objective results are "rational" by external standards. The implication of this postulate for macroeconomic policy and politics in general is enormous because the limits of human knowledge also belong to the authorities. Austrian economics condemns the "Pretense of Knowledge" (1974) of the fatal deceit of the authorities that claim to know better than the individual themselves and believe that markets must be subject to public control.

By making human action the central theme of economics, various aspects that are specific of the Austrian approach come into focus. Foremost among them are individualism, time, sequence, uncertainty, and adaptation. If one must distinguish the Austrian school by one major criterion, it would be "human action", and this concept would stand in contrast to "equilibrium". The concept of "human action" is the distinguishing factor that separates Austrian economics from "neoclassical formalism" and the hypostatization of Keynesian aggregate analysis.

For the Austrian economist, averages and aggregates cannot serve as determinants, and they do not allow for the establishment of causal relationships. It is scientifically invalid to establish causal relationships among statistical concepts. Such an approach would impose the inadequate model of the natural sciences on the study of humans as they act in the economic, political, and societal environment.

In the words of Hayek (1995):

> To me it seems as if this whole effort (of econometrics) were due to a mistaken effort to make the statistically observable magnitude the main object of theoretical explanation. But the fact that we can statistically ascertain certain magnitudes does not make them causally significant, and there seems to me no justification whatever in the widely held conviction that there must be discoverable regularities in the relation between those magnitudes on which we have statistical information. Economists seem to have come to believe that since statistics represent the only quantitative data which they can obtain, it is these statistical data which are the real facts with which they deal and that their theories must be given such a form that they explain what is statistically ascertainable. There are of course a few fields, such as the problems of the relation between the quantity of money and the price level, where we can obtain useful approximations to such simple relations— though I am still not quite persuaded that the price level is a very useful concept. But when it comes to the mechanism of change, the chain of cause and effect which we must trace in order to be able to understand the general character of the changes to be expected, I do not see that the objectively measurable aggregates are of much help.

Although Austrians may agree that economics deals with choice (Buchanan 1969), the Austrian approach does not concentrate on choice per se, but on the logic of human action, which implies choice but also transcends it. The concept of decision-making, for example, which dominates modern economics, is very limited, as it suggests that human beings confront predominantly an intellectual task when making choices. Human action has a wider scope. It has to be understood as an active choice that goes beyond calculation. Action involves the human being in the completeness of his existence including his existence in time. Because human action involves the person in his whole existence, time and expectations about future settings play an essential role, and the process of subjective evaluation goes beyond short-term maximization and will necessarily include a range of values and the longer term. "Action aims at change and is therefore in the temporal order... He who acts distinguishes between the time before the action, the time absorbed by the action, and the time after the action has been finished. He cannot be neutral with regard to the lapse of time".

Value and rationality are intimately linked to individual subjectivity. Human action is guided by meaning; it is anchored in the thinking of the individual and as such it contains the tendency to err. That markets fail (with respect to the criteria of the nirvana theory of neoclassical equilibrium analysis) is as obvious as the observation that any human action is often erroneous, which makes constant adaptation a necessity. But that is the reason why the power of planning is limited and central planning is a failure. When Austrian economics favors the market economy, it is because of this theoretical perspective, which sees markets as the best available means to guide individual adaptation and to generate knowledge. However, it would be wrong to presume that for Austrian economics markets are necessarily ubiquitous and to assume that economic calculation must be necessary in all aspects of human life. Besides markets, there exists the power of politics (including force) along with ideologies and traditions, which also influence individual thinking and human action. The rationality of human action does not disappear when an individual is confronted with the conflict between his family's tradition and his personal aspirations, for example. The recognition of the trade-off itself is an act of rationality. Radical subjectivism and individualism do not exclude non-economic behavior or denounce it as irrational. Human valuation is subjective, and the individual regards certain purposes as beyond the realms of commerce. While economic reasoning covers large parts of human existence, it does not cover all aspects of life.

3   Uncertainty and Contingency

Among the three basic ways of coping with the uncertainty of the future—gambling, speculation, and engineering—speculation is the adequate form for human action when dealing with economic and financial matters.

Speculation is the basic mode of entrepreneurial judgment. But the desire for apparently exact prediction and for establishing simple rules drives the mathematical economist toward idealizations and forms of modeling, which represent economic problems as if they were gambling events or engineering tasks. Speculation as entrepreneurial judgment would be unnecessary if the future were not uncertain. Then it would be possible to calculate the future structure of the market and economics could be turned into a forecasting profession like an exact science. Yet, as Mises points out:

> The entrepreneurial idea that carries on and brings profit is precisely that idea which did not occur to the majority. It is not correct foresight as such that yields profits, but foresight better than that of the rest. The prize goes only to those dissenters who do not let them be misled by the errors accepted by the multitude. What makes profits emerge is the provision for future needs for which others have neglected to make adequate provision. (ibid., p. 867)

In this view, it is futile to base economic decisions on formulas. Human action in the economy must use relative prices as the guideposts for making plans, but information and the numbers which appear as prices do not speak for themselves and instead must be assessed, compared, and finally related to one's personal value system. The same crude bit of information has various shades of meaning for different persons and quite often it is of a very different quality as to its practical relevance. Prices cannot substitute judgment. They are tools to make judgments.

For Austrian economics, the market process is an "indissoluble intertwinement of actions and reactions" (ibid., p. 333) based on diverse subjective valuations and on the huge variety of individual plans all of which are not directly observable beyond the resulting connection of prices. This structure of relative prices, however, does not reflect agreement on valuations, but the observable exchange ratios in the market are the product of a discrepancy in attributing values. Prices, although they convey information, do not imply that these are correct or "efficient".

In addition, what is usually called "present prices" reflects the conditions of the past, and past prices are of little value for entrepreneurial valuation:

> The prices of the past do not influence the determination of future prices. It is, on the contrary, the anticipation of future prices that determines the state of prices of the complementary factors of production. The determination of prices has, as far as the mutual exchange ratios between various commodities are concerned, no direct causal relation whatever with the prices of the past. The allocation of the nonconvertible factors of production among the various branches of production and the amount of capital goods available for future production are historical magnitudes; in this regard the past is instrumental in shaping the course of future production and in affecting the prices

of the future. But directly the prices of the factors of production are determined exclusively by the anticipation of future prices of the products. (ibid., p. 333)

Equilibrium in terms of fulfillment of expectations is temporary at best. By their very nature, market prices are necessarily volatile as they reflect the uncertainty of our expectations that is even more pronounced when it comes to the valuation of assets. Governments that presume that due to a position of authority they could do away with this instability base their cause on the belief that bureaucracies are better equipped to deal with the uncertainties of the future than the individual entrepreneurs and the individual consumers. By doing so, they discard the essence of markets.

Governmental market interventions mislead the adaptation process of individual actors. They add further elements of uncertainty to the formation of expectations and frustrate anticipated courses of action. The popularity of interventionism—defined as the efforts of political authorities to reallocate resources other than in a free market—can easily be explained in terms of political interests. Epistemologically, however, interventionism stands on very weak grounds once the assumption of determinism is loosened.

While it is widely acknowledged how direct interventions disrupt individual product markets, macroeconomic intervention and the stabilization of price levels and currency markets continue to be regarded as prime tasks for economic policy. But the unresolved methodological and practical problems of interventionism apply also to macroeconomic stabilization policies. Macroeconomic aggregates are ill-defined concepts and of dubious statistical validity. The conceptual units that are used in macroeconomic policy are statistical constructs and their presumed causal connection lacks reliability. Other than when believing in mystical forces is it methodologically invalid to speak of causal relationships among macroeconomic aggregates or averages without referring to the micro-level, that is, human action.

It is methodologically invalid to transfer the conclusion that the market model is deficient to markets as real-world phenomena and additionally imply that corrective governmental measures are warranted. The undisputed fact that product and financial markets are imperfect in the light of the theory of perfect competition does not imply that the actions of market participants were "irrational", and less so is the conclusion appropriate that therefore state intervention would be required. There is a huge difference between the type of statement that determines the specific outcome of a system and that which refers to the general properties of a system. Economic theory can determine the general properties of the market system. No economics that is known to a human being can deliver what the interventionist would need to know to justify policy: the specific result of a certain market constellation and the way the intervention would specifically alter the outcome.

When comparing the Austrian or praxeological approach with the perfectionist ideal of the efficient market theory and the thesis of human irrationalism, it turns out that praxeology avoids both traps of, first, assuming that financial markets were always efficient and, second, postulating that market prices are the outcome of the psychopathological behavior of frenzied madmen.

The promoters of "stabilization policies" ignore that error necessarily forms a part of human action. They will never completely disappear from human life. In a world where the future is unknown the occurrence of errors—or disequilibria when defined in terms of the fulfillment of expectations—is an integral of human action in a complex and dynamic environment with innumerous interactions. Unhampered markets receive their privileged status in this context not from the chimera of being perfect but because they allow continuous adaptation, that is, the constant correction of errors as they are identified by subjective valuations.

In a market economy there is no such thing as certainty about the future prices. The status of wealth, which is attributed to a certain arrangement of capital goods by the market process, is always at stake. There is a constant process of re-pricing of capital goods at work. In a world of unexpected change, Ludwig Lachmann (1991, p. 676) once remarked, "it is most unlikely that the same man will continue to be right in his guesses about possible new uses for existing or potential resources time after time, unless he is really superior. And in the latter case his heirs are unlikely to show similar success—unless they are superior, too." In capitalism there is no need for state-controlled redistribution, because under conditions of free markets, "the maintenance of wealth is always problematical; and in the long run it may be said to be impossible" (Lachmann, ibid.).

The market process is the great leveler because in a market economy "a process of redistribution of wealth is taking place all the time before which those outwardly similar processes which modern politicians are in the habit of instituting, pale into comparative insignificance, if for no other reason than that the market gives wealth to those who can hold it, while politicians give it to their constituents who, as a rule, cannot".

For Austrian economics the dramatic failure of socialism is no surprise. Overconfidence in financial and monetary stability and the anticipation of specific outcomes has become one of the most hideous pitfalls when it comes to decision-making in business, finance, and politics; it is a belief which has confused many otherwise brilliant minds and has trapped the public again and again.

4   Property and Markets

Human action uses economic calculation as a means. Economics as a part of the general theory of human action refers to choice. It would be wrong, however, to assume that the act of choice itself was calculation. Preferring a over b and b over c does not change by substituting a for 8 p, b for 15 r, and c for 7 p. The act of choice is still a ranking process. Only the introduction of money would allow making proper economics calculation.

For Mises it is important to note that it is only money and markets that allow rational calculation (capitalist accounting). Calculation in a society without money and markets is pure fiction. In this context, calculation is not abstract but refers to money expressed in numbers. The meaningful use of concepts such as "capital", "profit", and "loss", as well as "consumption", "savings", or "investment", requires their representation as monetary numbers. Any other use is highly fictitious and may be used only for illustrative purposes or for specific analytic purposes as a means of contrasting. Economic calculation as it is done in capitalist accounting is the unifying principle of a market economy and represents the prime instrument of choice, but it is not choice. Economic calculation beyond a market economy and in its respect to the individual consumer and entrepreneur is a senseless effort. For something to have a monetary value means nothing more than being able to ascertain its historic or expected price, that is to say that it was sold and bought at this price in the past or that it might be sold at this price in the future. To be meaningful, economic calculation requires as preconditions: division of labor, private property for the means of production, and market exchange based on money. With the thesis that only monetary calculation in the context of these conditions makes it praxeologically useful, the Austrian theory is in opposition to an approach, which concentrates on "direct" (money-less) exchange or abstracts from the essential conditions of monetary market economy. In this respect, large parts of classical and neoclassical economic reasoning are fundamentally wrong or meaningless for the problems of a monetary market economy.

The individual time horizon for action varies and is different from one person to the next. Human action in time is based on the choice between earlier or later and follows the fundamental praxeological law of time preference. Human valuation takes place in the presence although the time horizon of individual valuation may go beyond one's lifetime and even toward eternity. The orientation toward the future results from the principle of human action, and preference-ranking pertaining to the future is its necessary condition. Any human act involves sequence and thus implies a ranking process that extends into the future.

Economic action must take into regard that production takes time and that there are differences in the usage-time of different goods. Money is the essential means for being able to make such comparisons, although calculation by itself does not mean valuation, which is always subjective.

In the process of production, physical capital is used up and finally vanishes, and with the satisfaction of past demands, new demands arise. In the process of production, new production methods may be found, making current physical production goods obsolete. This implies a constant transformation of physical capital and along with it goes a continuous process of varying valuations. Therefore, concepts like the preservation of capital, and, along with it, saving and investment, only make sense when they are based on monetary calculation. Individually, saving is the excess of production over consumption, but the physical content of production and consumption do constantly change.

While the meaning of saving is evident for an individual when used as money income minus spending for consumption, it becomes void of economic meaning when applied to the whole of the economy. It is misleading to value a newly applied capital good (investment) other than relating it to expected profits. It is also misleading to speak of "periods" when production and consumption in a market economy are continuous processes, where constantly new and different production processes are being applied and where valuations change along with the change of data. The conventional macroeconomic approach is blind to one of the most important sources of saving (and dissaving). Only from the individual perspective, and based on monetary calculation, does it appear that capital formation is also possible without reducing current consumption due to new discoveries of salable natural products and the implementation of production processes with higher productivity in the production of saleable goods. In addition, a different institutional framework, which improves the capitalist environment, a higher net result allows for an enlarged capital base without foregoing consumption. The constructive versus the destructive institutional and political forces that work against capital formation become obscured in the macroeconomic perspective. Systematic capital destruction can go along with high growth and high investment as macroeconomic accounting cannot differentiate between valuable and wasteful activities. Government intervention, credit allocation in the "public interest", soft budgets, and bailout guarantees, along with excessive money creation and fiscal dirigisme, are the common policy features that distort individual economic calculation and work toward the destruction of capital—although for some time the application of these policies may be accompanied by seeming prosperity.

Monetary calculation is essential for making rational economic plans in a system of division of labor. But this method can operate effectively only in a setting of certain social institutions, that is, an "institutional setting of the division of labor and private ownership of the means of production in which goods and services of all orders are bought and sold against a generally used medium of exchange, i.e., money".

5   Methodological Aspects

The Austrian approach to economics is "causal-realist" (Salerno 2007). The basic element of the economy is human action. From this perspective it follows that the range of knowledge is limited and human well-being is best served with a system that is inherently self-correcting as it is with competitive markets based on private property rights. Changes in data cause individual adaptation and these take place in time beginning with the identification and valuation of data changes and including the effects of intended and unintended consequences. This is where economic analysis comes into play as an instrument of human action. While not much specific knowledge is needed to know about the immediate consequences of data changes, economics as a scientific endeavor is needed when the long-run effects may deviate from those of the short run. The praxeological reason for the existence of a form of inquiry called "economics" results from the insight that only systematic investigation will generate the knowledge that informs about the deviations of the long-term consequences from the short-term results. This task requires sequential analysis. The central aspects that guide the sequential process of economic analysis are located in the basic elements of human economic activity—such as subjectivism of valuation, economic calculation, and relative prices. In this view, the inherent property of human action is the incompleteness of knowledge on which it is based. In the Austrian perspective it is the very essence of human action to go wrong. Action takes place in time, it is sequential, and while action takes place, data change. The conditions of the future deviate from the past, and they must be different from expected results because otherwise men would not go on to act. In this sense, current market prices are always "wrong". Otherwise, they would not change. Prices express expectations and thus relate to the future. It is the error about "equilibrium conditions" which makes prices change. Disequilibrium is the cause of human action. Based on human action, the focus of the Austrian theory is not directed to equilibrium but rather to the process of adaptation. The construct of an equilibrium situation does have significance as an analytic point of reference, but it must be kept in mind that equilibrium situations are mere constructs and have no existence outside of the model. Economic behavior is a continuous process of corrective action. To investigate this adaptation process, which leads to the formation of a new relation between prices, non-monetary exchange theorems are of little help. Monetary calculation by consumers and producers is the unifying principle of the market; it is the link that connects all its parts. Profit and loss in their monetary expression are the guiding principles of action in a market economy. Economic analysis must consider that individual action in a monetary market economy is based on current relative prices, and an economic analysis that "abstracts" from monetary prices is an inadequate tool of inquiry when it is to be applied in a meaningful way to an economy that makes use of wide-scale division of labor. Economic analysis in the Austrian tradition is the sequential analysis of relative prices as they emerge from individual human action in the context of a monetary exchange economy. From this perspective the analysis receives its meaningfulness and analytical concepts. Void of human action, economic terms tend to become empty and lose their connection with practical issues. As Mises points out:

> In asserting the a priori character of praxeology we are not drafting a plan for a future new science different from the traditional sciences of human action. We do not maintain that the theoretical science of human action should be aprioristic, but that it is and always has been so. Every attempt to

reflect upon the problems raised by human action is necessarily bound to aprioristic reasoning. It does not make any difference in this regard whether the men discussing a problem are theorists aiming at pure knowledge only or statesmen, politicians, and regular citizens eager to comprehend occurring changes and to discover what kind of public policy or private conduct would best suit their own interests.

In a misplaced effort to imitate the natural sciences, large parts of modern economics practice constructivism, whereby statistical aggregates serve as mental constructs and are put at the center of the investigation. In a variety of models, averages and aggregates are supposed to have an existence of their own outside of human action, and these entities are then supposed to animate the system. It is no wonder that there are many definitional problems that plague mainstream macroeconomics in determining these quantitative aggregates even when their statistical exactness, such as with monetary aggregates, is very high. Definitional exercises of this kind must not be confounded with the strife for exactness of measurement that characterizes the natural sciences. In mainstream macroeconomics it is rather so that if one construct does not properly work, it must be redefined until it finally fits. The ideal is to construct the economy as a machine with the government function as the machine master. In their conclusion, these models make the behavior of consumers and businessmen deterministic, while the government is the only agent left to act as it had a free will. It was not so long ago when the hubris of mainstream macroeconomics was at its peak with the claim that the machine economy could be accelerated and slowed down at will by proper government policies.[1] In this perspective, the government remains seen as an idealized benevolent despot that performs its policies for the common good. It took

---

[1] Paul A. Samuelson, for example, deemed it for certain in 1956 to say that "economic science is not only neutral to the question of the desired rate of capital accumulation—it is also neutral as to the ability of the economy to realize any decided-on rate of capital formation. I repeat: With proper fiscal and monetary policies, our economy can have full employment and whatever rate of capital formation and growth in wants." In 1962, Samuelson put forth the thesis: "We no longer regard cyclical swings as immutable facts of nature, like the inevitable plagues that man could do nothing about before the age of penicillin, sulpha, medical care and public health. Fiscal and monetary policies can ameliorate, moderate, and perhaps even compensate fully for such tendencies toward sluggish investment opportunities." Quotes in: George M. Furstenberg and Jin-Ho Jeong, Owning up to Uncertainty in Macroeconomics, in: The Geneva Papers on Risk and Insurance, Vol. 13, No. 46, January 1988, pp. 12–90.

public choice theories, which came into prominence only in the late 1970s to reject this claim (Rowley 2004).

Austrian economics holds that this approach does not work for the social sciences, and even if it should work, the results will be mediocre at best. The reason for this is that we already know the basic elements of human action. The categories of praxeological thinking are directly given to us, because human action is common to all men as human beings. Ends and means are fundamental categories of human action, while the elements of natural objects can only be known empirically. Therefore, the direction of investigation in the social sciences must be reverse to that of the natural sciences. In the natural sciences we usually know the whole of a natural object before we ascertain its parts. Therefore, the natural way of inquiry must be reductionism. But for the social world, on the other hand, we know what human action is, and we know that markets and money do not exist outside of human action and apart from meaning. What we do not know are the resulting complexities because of the manifold interrelated human actions. These complex phenomena cannot be grasped easily. One cannot observe a market or investment without relating them to human action and to human meaning. Money is not just a piece of printed paper. The theory of human action is needed to explain what is going on and why markets, money, or investments do exist—with "ends" and "means" representing the central category of explanation.

In the perspective of Austrian economics, science itself is a praxeological concept and such directly tied to human action. Science is the refined and systematic way of the practical approach to objects (including the human body). In this process of study, technology and science go hand in hand, and both, science and technology, are *praxeology* applied to the areas of human interest. Science is a form of human action. In the perspective of praxeology, the method of the natural sciences as reductionism is indeed the appropriate form of dealing with the outer world. Be it the weather or the fall of the apple from a tree are phenomena that are fully accessible to human observation. Yet how these events come about is not known in a direct way. In contrast to these areas of the external world, the basic constituents of human action are well known to the individual, but its outcome as social and economic phenomena are highly complex in the totality of their interactions. Yet for the study of human action itself reductionism is inadequate. Here, we must start with simple essential abstractions (which are easy to make such as man acts) to the more complex abstractions that will come closer to reality (which are difficult to achieve) with the idea of explaining total or at least a large part of complexity.

As elaborated by Hayek in his later works (see Klein 1992), the Austrian approach ultimately leads to constitutional political economy, that is, it offers a set of principles for the constitutional elements of an economic order directed at attaining and preserving individual liberty and economic productivity. Austrian economics, based on methodological individualism and subjectivity of valuations, provides a series of guiding posts for economic policy that tend to be put aside by mainstream economics. Foremost among these principles, which can be deducted in a systematic way from the main principle of human action, ranks the principle of free markets along with a monetary order that is not subject to government or central bank intervention and that is not exposed to the volatilities of fiduciary money creation of the banking sector. Austrian economics rejects government ad hoc interventions yet there is a difference between the anarcho-libertarian position which rejects any kind of government role and the ordo-libertarian position, which rejects ad hoc interventionism but accepts the state's role as a guarantor of institutions that favor personal and economic liberty.

In this perspective, the research orientation of Austrian economics becomes mainly institutional. The basic question of inquiry thus becomes: which institutions promote individual liberty such as to allow the attainment of individual prosperity and its diffusion to society as a whole in the forms of capital accumulation and technological progress?

CHAPTER 3

Money and Monetary Policy

Abstract This part treats the contrast between conventional monetary policy and the Austrian approach. The starting point is the concept of money as a tool to facilitate economic exchange and as an indispensable instrument of rational economic calculation. In the praxeological perspective, the interest rate is intimately linked to time preference. From that it follows that monetary policy creates havoc when the policy rate of interest deviates from its natural rate. Austrian economics treats money and inflation fundamentally different from conventional macroeconomics and rejects on this basis current central banking and aggregate demand management. Conventional macroeconomic theory and policy stand in contrast to the Austrian macroeconomics which offers a proper well-developed theory of the business cycle that differentiates between a productivity-led economic expansion and a credit-driven boom-and-bust sequence.

Keywords Money • Prices • Inflation • Central banking •
Macroeconomic demand management • Boom-and-bust

© The Author(s), under exclusive license to Springer Nature
Switzerland AG 2024
A. P. Mueller, *A Primer on Austrian Macroeconomics*,
Palgrave Studies in Austrian Economics,
https://doi.org/10.1007/978-3-031-75189-9_3

1   Purpose and Origin of Money

Money developed as a general medium of exchange to solve the problem of the double coincidence of needs. Without a universal means of payment, the exchange of goods would be very limited. Without money as an intermediary of exchange, people are faced with the problem of finding an exchange partner who not only wants the good one offers for sale, but this potential buyer would also have to be in possession of the specific good that one himself does demand. Without money, not all beneficial transactions can be realized. The use of money as an exchange agent opens the possibility that the prospective seller will find more potential buyers for the goods on offer and that the buyers with the highest willingness to pay can be identified. Money is therefore a prerequisite for price formation, which in turn makes it possible for the satisfaction of more urgent needs expressed by willingness to pay to be given priority.

Driven by the human desire to improve personal well-being, individual economic interest will motivate individuals to exchange their goods for another good, even if they do not intend to use this good for their own immediate consumption purposes. People act in this way in the expectation of reselling the good they have received in exchange to finally obtain the commodity they are looking for consumption. Preference is given to those goods as general barter goods that are widely accepted in exchange and can thus be easily exchanged for other goods. Then, also influenced by habit, a certain number of goods are used more frequently and willingly in exchange. Eventually, the use of a particular good or a limited number of goods will emerge as a commonly used medium of exchange.

Historically, markets are created to facilitate barter. Without a plan or official guidance, certain goods emerge as a generally accepted means of payment. For this to happen over time, there is no need for a statutory obligation or a separate consideration of the public interest. The origin of the money is thus located in the economic process itself and is not determined by the state or other legislation.

Money is not the product of a formal agreement, and it was not introduced by a state legislature. The origin of money is economic in nature and has shown itself over time in different places depending on the prevailing economic situation. The origin of money lies in the increasing insight that by giving up less marketable commodities for those of greater marketability, their special economic purposes are promoted by a significant step, and thus money arose in numerous independent cultural centers with the progressive development of the national economy.

The commodity (or group of goods) that becomes money results from practical usefulness. As Carl Menger emphasizes in his *Principles of Economics* (1871), it would be a mistake to assume that the function of money as such is "a measure of value" or serves the purpose of "preserving value". These functions are accidental to the nature of money and are not included in the concept of "money proper". In the exchange of goods, there are no equivalents in the objective sense, and therefore money cannot serve as a measure of exchange value.

The actual function of money lies in its role as an intermediary of exchange and must not be equated with the concept of "legal tender" or misunderstood as a "store of value". Retaining money is not a function inherent in money. The savings function is rather derived from the function of money as a medium of exchange. As the monetary economy progresses, accumulation is increasingly being replaced by capitalization, the accumulation of productive goods.

With these explanations, Carl Menger draws attention to aspects of money that are widespread as misconceptions about the function of money. It is not uncommon to believe that one is storing value by saving money. Indeed, the misconception is widely spread that one would store some kind of value when investing in financial assets for future pension benefits. Properly understood, however, such savings are not money in its proper sense because its value as a means of exchange lies in the future and cannot be determined beforehand. One does not know in the present how much and which goods can be obtained with a specific monetary unit in the time to come. If the money that has been saved loses all or part of its function as an intermediary of exchange because it is no longer generally accepted, it becomes apparent that no accumulation of value has taken place. Money has no inherent function as a store of value. Only through its function as an exchange mediator does the "value" of money prove itself.

Many other misconceptions about money follow from the mistaken belief that money is a state institution. As Menger further explains in a separately published work on the subject of the concept of "money" (1892), money as an intermediary of exchange originally did not come into being through law or convention, but through "habit", that is, through a similar action of individuals living together in society (as the unintended result of specific-individual efforts of the members of society) that corresponds to the same individual motivations and advances in the intelligence of the humans and finally becomes generally used through progressive imitation as it happens likewise with language, for example. Like other institutions that arose spontaneously, money can also be promoted as an intermediary of exchange by legislation—but it can also happen that the legislature hinders its automatic development.

Money is not a state invention, nor is it the product of a legislative act, and the sanction of the same on the part of the state authority is therefore alien to the concept of money altogether. The existence of certain commodities as money has also naturally arisen from economic conditions, without the need for state influence. This circumstance of natural development, as in the case of other institutions that have arisen in a similar way, does not preclude their influence by the state and as they can be perfected by state and adapted to the diverse and changing needs of the economic interaction, government can also corrupt the original function of money.

In the historical beginnings of economic activity, people's interest was directed less to exchange value than to use value. People were looking for goods that served as the immediate satisfaction of needs. But with economic development, the exchange value of a good increasingly enters into the interest of people. The problem arises that people must find each other with opposing estimates of exchange value so that A has to offer for sale the good X that Y wants, while B offers the specific good X that A desires. In an economy without money, development is hindered because the person willing to exchange must find an exchange partner who not only offers the goods he is looking for, but who must also be the one who needs the goods offered.

The solution to this problem arises through the fact that different goods have different degrees of marketability. As every market observer knows, there are great differences in the ease with which the different types of goods can be exchanged in terms of their tradability. In addition to the limits imposed on trade regarding the persons to whom a particular good can be sold, the marketability of a good also depends on the location where the trade takes place and on the quantity that is offered and demanded on the market. In addition to the size of the market, the durability of the good also determines its marketability. These aspects are fundamental to the use of money as an intermediary of exchange.

In order for the exchange to take place, A must value the worth of the exchange good Y higher than the exchange good X, while the opposite assessment is required for B, that is, the latter must value the good Y higher than the good X. Direct exchange is inhibited by the fact that there must be a "double coincidence of needs" in order to realize it.

Without money, there would be no exchange of goods between A, B, and C, because although A offers the good X that B demands, B does not have the good Y that A wants to exchange. Similarly, C has the good Y that A demands, but not the good X that B wants.

With the introduction of money as a general medium of exchange, the problem of double coincidence is solved. A sells his goods X to buyer B, who pays with money. A buys property Y from C with money, and C can buy from B property Z, which he wishes to acquire, in return for money. It is through money that the full potential of the productive advantage of specialization can happen.

Money is productive because it enables the exchange of goods and services that would otherwise be omitted. The use of money in commercial transactions is beneficial for market participants. With the development of money-mediated barter, markets are created on which price formation takes place. The monetary market prices increase the level of information provided to market participants about the existing market situation. This is another advantage that comes with the use of money. The larger the market, the more specialization becomes possible and rewarding. The existence of a monetary economy is thus a fundamental prerequisite for the increase in productivity and thus of economic prosperity.

The function proper to money is that of a commonly used intermediary of exchange. The "exchange value" expressed in money, its so-called money value of the goods, which appears as "price", merely represents an exchange relationship between the purchased goods and money.

For the general concept of money, it is irrelevant whether money acquires its function automatically or by coercion. In this sense, there is good or bad money, healthy or pathological money, money that is automatically or state-designed and perfected or corrupted by the state. Governments tend to disregard the central function of money for economic prosperity. They treat money as if it were in fact merely a product of human convenience in general and legislative arbitrariness in particular. This legislative-interventionist attitude with which governments typically approach money has also influenced monetary theory and contributed a lot to encouraging errors about the nature of money. State intervention deteriorates the quality of money (Bagus 2020) if it is misused for purposes that go beyond its actual function as an intermediary of exchange. Carl Menger, as the founder of Austrian economics, could not have imagined the extent to which the misuse of money began less than half a century after the publication of his *Principles* when the gold peg was lifted at the beginning of World War I in 1914.

A little more than 30 years after the end of the gold standard, Keynesianism has theoretically legitimized the corruption of money. As enthusiastically as this theory of money abuse has been taken up by politicians, it is currently happening with the so-called Modern Monetary Theory (Mueller 2020). Playing fast and loose with money has been the standard now for more than a century. In disregard of the actual function of money, immense prosperity is sacrificed to the apparent advantages of monetary. The quality of money determines the extent to which money can perform its welfare-promoting function. In disregard of this fact, money is misused for purposes that are alien to the actual function of money as an intermediary of exchange.

For Austrian economics, the function of money is to facilitate exchange. It is a means of payment. As such, it is also an instrument for economic calculation. The value of money lies in the promotion of productivity and thus of prosperity. Austrian economics denounces sharply the corruption of money as it shows up in the tolerance for price inflation by the authorities.

2   THE VALUE OF MONEY

An important distinction must be made between the changes in the price level and of the change in relative prices. The price level changes because of the variation in the relation between the amount of money and the volume of goods in an economy. Relative prices change because of the variations in demand and supply in the market. The price level results from the relation between the amount of money and the supply of goods. In contrast, relative prices reflect demand and supply for specific goods.

If the money supply is constant, the increase in the supply of goods would bring about a benevolent deflation. Yet often the monetary authorities expand the money supply more than the economy can produce goods and the result is a general price inflation. Relative prices are indispensable to guide the behavior of consumers and investors, while price inflation is a constant risk factor for entrepreneurial decision-making because it affects both the level and the structure of prices. Because the price level impacts upon relative prices, misallocations happen in the economy. A rising or falling "price level" does not mean that all goods rise or fall equally. Inflation and deflation increase the variation of the relative prices.

In order for prices to fulfill their function as instruments of information and incentive, they must be flexible and responsive to changes in demand and supply. The concept of "price stability" is a misplaced notion for this type of price change. When the central bank speaks of price stability, the term does not refer to relative prices, but to the price level.

The published "consumer price index" and the other price indices represent a statistical hodgepodge. One can concoct such statistics in many ways, and one can do this without violating common statistical rules. The so-called hedonic calculation, which attempts to take account of quality changes of the goods, is just one example.

Yet despite all the statistical tricks that are being invented and applied, the core issue remains unresolved: what is being measured by purchasing power and what is the value of money—other than subjective and individualistic—upon which one could base the calculation?

Along with the statistics related to the figures about the domestic and national product, the price index is one of the most unreliable, most deceiving, and most abused statistical economic numbers. This is the case because the price index provides the basis for a series of other statistical indicators as it serves as a deflator and enters economic growth and productivity figures.

These macroeconomic numbers suffer from the illusion that one could observe the properties of an object—called "the economy"—and could then measure as if they were physical objects. Whatever finesse is applied to their calculation to make these statistics more accurate, it cannot do away with their basic invalidity that results from the impossibility of getting a fixed standard of measurement for value.

Attempts to measure the economy as if it were an object have their origin in government planning. Treating the economy as a whole becomes necessary for socialist central planners and for a war economy. Price indices and other statistics about macroeconomic variables are needed when some center with decision-making power wants to control all or most of the economy. Both fathers of modern national income accounting, John Richard Nicholas Stone (Nobel Prize in Economics 1984) and Simon Kuznets (Nobel Prize in Economics in 1971) served in war planning offices where they developed and refined the concepts. The results of these planning endeavors are well known, but while socialist-type total economic planning is off the screen even for many devout socialists, central monetary planning by manipulating money, credit, and the exchange rate ranks still high on the public agenda. Central banking is the last refuge for those under the spell of the pretense of knowledge. Fixing their eyes on the so-called price stability" or following the inflation targeting schemes, central bankers try to hit not just a movable target but one that is more symbolic than real. This way, they neglect the inflationary expansion of money and debt.

As with individual prices, the prices of groups of goods and services rise and fall. There are always inflationary and deflationary areas in an economy. While the price index may signal stability, huge movements in both directions can happen with individual prices. When small aggregate price movements occur or when opposing forces are at work, the price index renders no valuable signal. If, however, strong tendencies in one or the other direction of the general price level are underway, and when this turns up in the price index, it is too late for the central banks to effectively control the "price level". Price indexes average out the extremes; they are unable to signal the subtler price movements, and they leave out relevant items such as asset prices. This way, it is not only so that the public is being deceived, but the central bankers also themselves are falling victim to their calculations.

As Ludwig von Mises (Human Action 1998, p. 218) explained:

> (t)he money equivalents as used in acting and in economic calculation are money prices, i.e., exchange ratios between money and other goods and services. The prices are not measured in money; they consist in money. Prices are either prices of the past or expected prices of the future. A price is necessarily a historical fact either of the past of the future. There is nothing in prices which permits one to liken them to the measurement of physical and chemical phenomena.

Adding up all sales or compounding all assets in an economy eliminates the meaning of prices. This kind of aggregation differs from what a company or a person does when one calculates the profits or the relative wealth position. When a person adds up the prices of his various assets, he gets a number about his current wealth relative to the price universe he selects as his point of reference. For a company, it is sales, costs, and profits that matter for the purpose of accounting. Neither for personal matters nor for business decisions macroeconomic figures are necessary. The authors of the national income accounting framework were aware of the shortcomings of their statistics. One can determine the weight of the overall output of certain types of steel, but one cannot, in the same way, come to a reasonable result by measuring in one number the aggregate production of automobiles, of refrigerators, or of personal computers—not to speak about the problems one confronts when one tries to add up the output of teachers, nurses, songwriters, or software programmers together with apples and oranges.

A company can count its production in terms of units of model M or T. If the company wants a figure for the total, it must resort to sales. Before sales, one can only enumerate how many units of each specific item category are in stock, and only by assuming that the company's products will catch certain prices, is it possible to calculate the expected monetary amount—but not the value of production.

Mises explained it this way: "Prices are always money prices, and costs cannot be taken into account in economic calculation if not expressed in terms of money. If one does not resort to terms of money, costs are expressed in complex quantities of diverse goods and services to be expended for the procurement of a product" (Mises, Human Action, p. 39). Likewise, one cannot add up values or valuations:

> Valuation can only arrange goods in scales of preference. It can never attach to a good something that could be called a quantity or magnitude of value. It would be absurd to speak of a sum of valuations or values. It is permissible to declare that, due allowance being made for time preference, the value attached to a product is equal to the value of the total complex of complementary factors of production. But it would be nonsensical to assert that the value attached to a product is equal to the "sum" of the values attached to the various complementary factors of production. One cannot add up values or valuations. One can add up prices expressed in terms of money, but not scales of preference. One cannot divide values or single out quotas of them. A value judgment never consists in anything other than preferring a to b. (Mises, Human Action, p. 332)

In a private market economy, the aims of economic activity are diverse and represent individual and subjective valuations. Each good and service has a different value for each user. There is no common standard of value available. This is even more so the case when new products and new kinds of services come to the market. Valuations not only are heterogeneous among persons but also differ for the same person according to his specific circumstances. Human beings have different needs and desires in different situations, and they experience changes in taste. Preferences themselves are experimental devices.

Quality is not an attribute inherent to the things, but it is a valuation, which is imputed to the goods and services by the economic actor. Economic action aims to improve one's condition and what makes up an amelioration is subject to continuous change. Therefore, there is no objective way to measure overall wealth in aggregate form without coarse distortions and without violating the basic principles of economic valuation. Market prices (Mises, Human Action, p. 699) "are not expressive of equivalence, but of a divergence in the valuation of the two exchanging partners", and the value attached to the unit of supply is subject to the law of diminishing marginal utility.

3   MONEY AND INTEREST

Economics as a part of the theory of human action deals primarily with a monetary economy based on the division of labor. Direct exchange and Robinson Crusoe models may serve as theoretical points of reference, but their fictitious character must be kept in mind. By focusing on money, Austrian economics contrasts strongly in relevance when compared to other models of economics. When applying its methodological principles to money, Austrian economics regards such phenomena as interest rates or the demand for money as the results of human valuation. The central focus of the Austrian theory of money is directed at the theory of interest, as it reflects most clearly the aspect of subjective valuation.

In its primary form, as the "originary" interest rate, this "Urzins" is the discount that human action must give to later available goods compared to the earlier available goods, which may render the same service. Otherwise, man would not act. By necessity, human action implies a preference for the immediate. Consumption closer to the present is valued higher than consumption later. To put it in another way, in an imaginary world without this original interest rate, saving would become infinite. On the other hand, an unlimited rise in this rate would finally eliminate saving. The difference between the primary and the monetary rate of interest becomes obvious when thinking about the elimination of interest income (by expropriation or taxation). Then, saving would stop and cause the consumption of accumulated capital as its consequence, precisely because the primary rate of interest cannot be removed from human valuation.

The central thesis of Mises' monetary theory consists in the proposition that the monetary rate of interest may deviate from the neutral rate due to money creation (or its contraction) in the credit markets. If the money rate falls below the neutral rate and thus deviates from the original rate of interest, the monetary rate will deviate from the original valuation between present and future goods, and as future goods have become relatively cheaper, the demand for them increases.

By using sequential analysis, the Misesian theory points out that money affects the economy heterogeneously. Money cannot be neutral because it enters the economy not at once nor at the same time, nor in the same quantities for all economic agents. While money may or may not change the price level, it always will change relative prices and with it the relative fortunes of individual economic agents. In the words of Mises:

> The essence of monetary theory is the cognition that cash-induced changes in the money relation affect the various prices, wage rates, and interest rates neither at the same time nor to the same extent. If this unevenness were absent, money would be neutral; changes in the money relation would not affect the structure of business, the size and direction of production in the various branches of industry, consumption, and the wealth and income of the various strata of the population.

The monetary rate of interest cannot be a neutral rate of interest in the sense that it would be the monetary expression of the original rate of interest, because changes in money affect prices not homogeneously and all prices at the same time. Money enters the economy at specific recipients and affects the rest of the economic actors in different ways. Even if the change in the quantity of money could be known in time, and if it were known for which kind of activities it enters the economy, it is impossible to know beforehand how this will affect the different prices. It is principally impossible to foresee how, when, and to what degree individual valuations will change. Only perfect foresight could transform the monetary rate of interest into a neutral rate by applying a price premium. However, the formation of expectations about a certain direction of prices is disparate and must remain uncertain.

This monetary theory based on individual valuation and sequential analysis leads to the Austrian theory of the business cycle, which holds that credit expansion and contraction bring about deviations of the monetary rate of interest from the primary rate, thus transmitting false signals and leading to misallocation between the production of immediate and future goods. Easy money creates an illusion of wealth and thus instigates an enlargement of the production process while consumers aspire for the acquisition of goods that rank higher in their time scale. In the boom period, for example, goods that were regarded as "luxuries" now appear to be within one's reach. But as the real wealth of the economy cannot be increased by money, disproportionalities occur within the economy, which later require reversals brought about by a recession.

4   Prices and Inflation

Without much thought whether it makes sense or not, "inflation" is officially defined as a general rise in prices. Official statistics claim that the "price level" can be measured and its change could be calculated as the so-called inflation rate. There is almost no critical evaluation of the reliability of these numbers. Rarely is it mentioned that these concepts are statistical constructs. They are published as "official numbers" and, as such, they are subject to governmental interests.

The fundamental problem with the calculation of the price level is the assumption that money would measure the value of goods. This approach confounds value with exchange ratios. Money prices do not reflect the value of a good and therefore they do not measure anything. Consequently, it also makes no sense to speak of a "price level".

Mises (Human Action, p. 59) explains:

> When people talk of a "price level," they have in mind the image of a level of a liquid which goes up or down according to the increase or decrease in its quantity, but which, like a liquid in a tank, always rises evenly. But with prices, there is no such thing as a "level." Prices do not change to the same extent at the same time. There are always prices that are changing more rapidly, rising or falling more rapidly than other prices.

Prices are different from value. Prices make only sense as price relations, as relative prices. As such, they serve the acting man as an orientation about the prevailing market conditions. Prices answer the question of which goods and services cost more and which alternatives cost less on the market compared to other goods. As such, prices are a market phenomenon and cannot arise meaningfully outside of markets. Prices emerge on the market as exchange ratios (for the details of its calculation, see Mueller 2021).

Relative prices indicate the prevailing conditions of relative scarcity. The price ratio is inversely proportional to the exchange ratios. For example, if one unit of good A exchanges for two units of good B, good A costs twice as much as good B in terms of the respective monetary units. As it is obvious with the absolute number of the price tags in different currencies, the price figure itself is irrelevant and makes only sense as the ratio to other prices.

Money serves as a general medium of exchange. It does not measure anything. Likewise, prices make only sense as price ratios. Because both the scale and the measuring object are subject to change, measurement is not possible.

The obsession with the "price level" has done much harm to the conduct of monetary policy. Most modern central banks practice so-called inflation targeting" (Martínez-García et al. 2021) without being fully aware that the inflation rate as their indicator is a chimera. By following this concept, central banks ignore that their guidepost is a phantom and additionally that the idea itself that the price level should rise steadily makes no economic sense. In the perspective of the monetary theory of the Austrian School, the consternation of the monetary policymakers in the face of their repeated failure is neither a surprise nor historically new. The official inflation rate misleads the central bankers as well as the financial market operators.

Every household, every person, and every region has its specific consumption patterns. Even if all buildings were of the same type, they would be different because of their location and would therefore have very different prices. Even when it comes to such a simple good as an egg, a closer look reveals that even with eggs, it is much more than size and color that distinguishes them.

The price index is a statistical illusion based on the chimera of a fixed basket of goods as a unit of measurement. There is no scientific method of measuring the price level. For a person who lives in his own house and has no plans to sell, neither the housing prices nor the height of the rents is of importance. The situation is similar to the stock market. Has the nation become richer when the stock market index has risen?

There is no such thing as the price level for the economy as a whole or the overall wealth of a society. Everyone has his own variations of the purchasing power of his money. What one can do is count the costs of one's own shopping cart and calculate its costs compared to one's income. Such a calculation shows whether the individual purchasing power has risen or fallen. To do this for an entire economy makes no sense. It is as futile a procedure as the common practice of calculating the overall economic wealth by summing up the prices for property, bonds, and stocks and claiming that this would represent national wealth.

Ludwig von Mises criticized the procedures of such macroeconomic calculations a long time ago when he wrote:

> All methods suggested for a measurement of the changes in the monetary unit's purchasing power are more or less unwittingly founded on the illusory image of an eternal and immutable being who determines by the application of an immutable standard the quantity of satisfaction which a unit of money conveys to him. It is a poor justification of this ill-thought idea that what is wanted is merely to measure changes in the purchasing power of money. The crux of the stability notion lies precisely in *this* concept of purchasing power.

Only pseudo-scales are available as a general evaluation. The assessment of the benefits of a product is subjective, or individual. The value of a good depends on the personal assessment of the changing circumstances. According to this subjective evaluation, the individual will make his choice according to the relative price changes.

Macroeconomic economic statistics are constructs. With the "inflation measurement", both the price as the object of the measurement and the market basket as the measuring rod undergo changes. Without a constant scale, no measurement is possible. What can be measured correctly is the money supply. Its change is the right use of the concept of "inflation" and the "inflation rate". Yet what appears to be an objective standard of measurement in the price statistics is the flawed effort to measure the unmeasurable. The numbers that get published as official inflation figures are very crude indicators at best. Taking these numbers at face value is naïve and harmful.

5   Critique of Central Banking

Since its inception, modern central banking has gone through various fashions and has adopted opposing paradigms. The US Federal Reserve System began its operations in 1914 and stood ready to provide the monetary conditions for financing the US entry into World War I, as the central bank did likewise in World War II and the many other military conflicts that were to follow. In Europe, the first consequence of the beginning of World War I was to abandon the gold standard and thus to turn the central banks into direct governmental tools.

In the early 1920s, the US central bank adopted the concept of maintaining a stable price level and consequently produced an economic boom that ushered the door to the Great Depression. In Europe, the Deutsche Reichsbank produced hyperinflation, and in the United Kingdom, the Bank of England tried in vain to bring the country out of a prolonged slump. In the 1930s, the deepening of the Great Depression made the US central bank try to re-inflate the system, but without success. By the early 1930s the political supremacy over central banking was completed. Irrespective of the degree of totalitarianism, the politicization of money encompassed the respective central banks from Moscow to Berlin and from Paris and France to Washington and Tokyo.

After World War II, there was a short period when the so-called Bretton Woods system was firmly in place with the establishment of a link of the US dollar to gold and a fixed exchange rate system with an adjustable peg for its member countries. In the 1960s, however, Keynesianism became the dominant doctrine of central banking. The US government ignored its obligation to limit the dollar emission to the size of its gold stock, and the US central bank put no breaks on the expansion of the money supply that ushered right into a decade of inflation first and stagflation later.

In West Germany, the newly founded "Bank deutscher Länder" (later called "Bundesbank") got its seat in Frankfurt in 1948 and not in the capital city, thereby signaling a certain symbolic detachment from politics. The law that created the new German central bank obliged monetary policy to pursue "price level stability". This clause, however, did not prevent that in the late 1960s and during the 1970s, inflation and then stagflation also hit Germany and other European countries. One reason for that was the existence of an international monetary system, which obliged the member countries to stabilize their exchange rates against the US dollar. While the foundation of this system was cast aside with the expansion of the mass of dollars, the Bundesbank, along with other central banks in Europe and the Japanese central bank, became the "buyers of the last resort" for the weakening greenback. The world experienced a massive increase in liquidity originating from the US dollar and spilling over to the other major currencies, as the central banks in Europe and in Japan bought dollars in exchange for their own currencies to stabilize the exchange rate. The consequence was "imported inflation". After a short liquidity-driven boost, the world economy slipped into the stagflation of the 1970s. While the first oil price shock worked as the catalyst of stagflation, the drastic increase in oil prices, however, must be seen as the result of the deteriorating dollar value.

The experience of stagflation led to a full turnaround of monetary policy in 1979/1980 when the US central bank embarked upon the monetarist experiment. However, inflation rates were brought down more by accident than according to plan. With the onset of the monetarist experiment, the velocity of money circulation, which had been trend-stable for decades, began to fall. Inadvertently, the restrictive monetary policy of the US Federal Reserve became more contractive than it was intended. Always ironic, history showed for monetary policy that as soon as monetarism got applied, one of its necessary conditions—the stability or at least trend-stability of the velocity of money—no longer held.

After that episode, the US central bank abandoned monetarism and turned to a pragmatic or rather an idiosyncratic approach. Under the chairmanship of Alan Greenspan from 1987 to 2006, US central banking became more and more a one-man show. Particularly during the second half of his term, Greenspan was not just a chairman of the Board of Governors of the Federal Reserve System, but he had become a guru and oracle in words and an avid bail-outer in deeds. During Alan Greenspan's reign, the dollar continued to lose purchasing power, yet there are people who call Greenspan one of the greatest central bankers of all time.

In Asia, meanwhile, the Japanese central bank produced first an unsustainable economic boom in the 1980s, then instigated the bust of 1989/1990, and then tried desperately but without success for more than a decade to re-inflate the economy by bringing down the policy rate of interest to zero. In the 1980s the Japanese central bank saw no need to worry in the face of booming stock and real estate markets because the price index remained relatively stable. The Bank of Japan boosted its monetary base in the late 1980s, then again in the late 1990s, and drastically since the end of 2012, each time contributing to the global liquidity glut. Japan provides an instructive example of a long period of stagnation caused by government policies. The Japanese economy has been in the economic slump for about 40 years, with economic weakness being linked to the stagnation of the economy's productivity.

Since the economic downturn began in the early 1990s, one government after another in Japan has been trying to escape the macroeconomic predicament with a policy of stimulating aggregate demand. The Bank of Japan massively supported this expansionist fiscal policy and pushed interest rates into negative territory. But despite this perfect Keynesian textbook policy, the economy has not picked up. As a legacy of this policy, Japan's public debt has grown to a dimension rarely reached outside of wartime.

Despite these enormous demand impulses, the Japanese economy did not come out of stagnation. Since the early 1990s, Japan's economic growth has not only been weak but also volatile. The legacy of Keynesianism that is now evident amounts to a huge debt overhang that has paralyzed private economic activity. Savings are declining, the fear of tax increases is increasing, and the zeal for innovation has waned. Instead of promoting a rapid recovery through the liquidation of bad investments, the policy measures have exacerbated the structural distortions of the economy. Macroeconomic policies since the 1990s have squandered much of the wealth that Japan amassed in the decades after World War II.

Japan is not the only country caught in the Keynesian trap. Since 2008, the United States and Europe have made similar mistakes. The Federal Reserve and the European Central Bank (ECB) have lowered interest rates, and governments have expanded their spending. However, these measures have not led to a solid economic expansion. The costs of such an economic policy are enormous. National debt is becoming a growing burden on the economy. Over time, the pace of productivity progress stalls even more, as it has already done in the United States and European countries over the past two decades. When the interest rate is pushed to zero and beyond, it leads to economic misallocation and distorts the distribution of income and wealth.

While the macroeconomic demand theory formulated by Keynes in his "General Theory" of 1936 is no longer the leading paradigm in economics faculties, it lives on as vulgar Keynesianism at the political level. There is still a widespread conviction in political circles that the economy needs an active stabilization policy and that monetary and fiscal incentives are necessary to achieve high economic growth, full employment, and a stable price level.

In Europe, a common currency, the euro, was introduced in 1999 and the statutes for the establishment of the European Central Bank called for utmost central bank autonomy and the priority of "price stability" of monetary policy. The seat of the European Central Bank is in Frankfurt, in equal distance to Brussels, where the executive branch of the European

Union is hosted, and Strasbourg, where the European Parliament resides. In contrast to the Bundesbank, whose statutes were actually simple law, the autonomy of the ECB has gained a kind of constitutional status and price level stability as its aimed is quasi-constitutionally sanctioned.

On February 1, 2006, Ben Bernanke took over the office as chairman of the Board of the Federal Reserve System. He has been known as a proponent of inflation targeting and an adherent to the idea that the task of a central bank is to maintain price level stability as measured by a price index. Bernanke announced "inflation targeting" as if it were something new when, in fact, it was invented—and later criticized—by Irving Fisher (1933) long ago.

The financial crisis of 2008 did not come from anywhere. Its basis was laid over a long period with the welfare state, the inflation of money, and the adoption of the Keynesian economic policy framework as the new orthodoxy. The great American boom since the 1980s was built on monetary expansion, low interest rates, and a relentless policy of bailouts when the bubbles burst. The result has been the build-up of unsustainable debt burdens. When debt accumulation hit its limit in the private sector and in the banking system, and when markets began to freeze, governments jumped in with bailout guarantees and stimulus packages, which only added a fiscal crisis on top of the financial market and economic crisis.

Excessive monetary expansion and the resulting low interest rates represent the immediate causes of the crisis of 2008. At a deeper level, however, lies the current monetary system. The structure that emerged after the breakdown of the Bretton Woods system in 1971 is cut off from an anchor. The new monetary schemes have become an engine of debt expansion in the private and public sectors. It is a system devoid of a mechanism that would curb debt expansion in time. The current monetary arrangements allow central banks to make the debt accumulation go on until the final collapse.

The crisis of 2008 and thereafter was as much a financial as an economic crisis and most of all it is a crisis of indebtedness. This excess of debt includes households and governments, and it includes the external balances, the persistent current account deficits of the United States, which, as their counterpart, imply the accumulation of surpluses in China and some other Asian and European countries.

With economic policies, there is often a considerable time lag between the phase when one plants the seeds and the phase when the harvest will come—between cause and effect. In the case of the financial and economic crisis of 2008, the time of planting goes back to the 1960s and 1970s when the welfare state became the new creed in the Western world, when economic policy adopted Keynesianism, and when the last remnants of the gold standard were removed. The late 1960s experienced the start of the drastic expansion of the welfare state, and in the early 1970s, the rest of what had remained of a sound monetary system was abandoned. Adopting the Keynesian economic policy model would make the triad complete. The new consensus encompasses an unhampered expansion of the welfare state, an activist discretionary monetary policy without anchor or definite rules, and the economic policy of vulgar Keynesianism with its false promise that the government had the tools to lift a country to prosperity and full employment through government spending and easy money.

It did not take long until this kind of policy produced its first disaster: stagflation. Facing the result of Keynesian politics in the rise of unemployment, economic stagnation, and inflation demand for a new economic policy paradigm arose, and it was found in "monetarism". Monetarism, however, as an economic policy concept, was in some respects an even more simplified version of Keynesianism. Despite its promotion of free markets, there was little true classical economics in the monetarist model. When monetarists declared, "We're all Keynesians now", it meant much more than an ironic twist.

When Reaganomics—the economic policy of President Ronald Reagan and his promotion to combine tax cuts and deregulation—came along in the early 1980s, this economic policy failed with its promise to reduce government expenditure. While the American central bank under its chairman Paul Volcker brought down the inflation rate and while unemployment fell, government deficits swelled and the public debt increased to new highs. That was the time when the slogan "deficits don't matter" emerged.

In this respect, the new economic policy proposition of "supply side economics" had become even more Keynesian. Now, the original idea of anti-cyclical public finance was put aside. The governments abandoned the principle that cuts of public expenditure and budget surpluses would be required in good economic times to have the funds to spend when the economy would turn into a recession. The new economic policy consensus says deficits would not matter and thus that one can ignore the debt levels and neglect the exchange rate of the dollar because central banks were held to be capable of managing the monetary side of the economy.

While a bailout may be beneficial in the individual case and is so for the persons who receive the bailout money, bailouts have systemic consequences: over time, each new bailout will add to the level of moral hazard, and after a series of bailouts, moral hazard will become systemic. What at first is a benign government gift, over time will become a manifest expectation, and bailouts will be nothing less than the rightful claims on government money.

Bailouts produce a moral hazard, and this way risk perception will diminish. Without the restraint of financial losses, an overexpansion of commercial activities will occur. Bailouts institutionalize perverse risk behavior, and it is not before long that the new aggressive attitude will rule across the board by the business community and by the financial market operators. In fact, bailouts impose a negative selection mechanism where prudence gets punished. With risk perception taken out of business life, the economic expansion means that a growing part of the resulting economic growth comes from unsustainable investments. This, in turn, implies that most of the economic activity that comes as the result of falling risk perception amounts to the squandering of capital. In relation to the point of departure, the economy that appears to be on the path of prosperity is getting poorer. When the bubble pops, the level of prosperity is lower than it was before the false boom.

The current international monetary system is more a "non-system" than a system or an order. It does not provide a sound monetary order. Interventionist systems, like the one that is now in existence for monetary matters, drive toward their own dissolution. It seems as if the end stage of the interventionist spiral has come full circle considering that the starting point of the modern interventionist state existed in getting hold of money creation. It is the sovereign authority over money that provides the conditions of the welfare-warfare state and the rise of the modern interventionist state.

The structure of the modern monetary system in combination with modern democracy produces the dynamics which drives toward price inflation and over-indebtedness. Deflation is the main concern of the monetary authorities because a falling price level means bankruptcy. Because of the irrational fear of deflation, the central bankers work as hard as they can to create debt inflation to lift the price level. Yet in as much as they succeed in promoting debt inflation, the final stage will be bankruptcy. Instead of letting the system go the shortcut to deflation and from there to bankruptcy, monetary authorities promote a detour from debt inflation to bankruptcy and from bankruptcy to deflation. Most of all, however, the modern interventionist policy measures are aimed at avoiding any recession and thus prone to prevent a re-positioning of the economy to correct the errors of the past concerning the capital structures.

Economic policy intervention in the form of bailouts creates a systemic moral hazard that for some time helped to avoid an economic downturn. Yet after that, there will be a collapse much harsher than anything that would have happened earlier if the policymakers had left the economy by itself to adapt.

The record of modern central banking is bleak. Even leaving aside such economic and consequently social disasters as those produced by the Weimar inflation and when only taking the blissful history of the United States as a prove, one can see that even here, the country with its central bank well in place has experienced more than ten years of depression in a stretch, various bouts of inflation, and more than a decade of stagflation. The US dollar has lost about 95 percent of its purchasing power since the Federal Reserve System was established.

6   Critique of Macroeconomic Demand Management

In the 1960s, Keynesianism became the dominant doctrine of central banking. Interest rates had to be low, so the mantra said, to stimulate investment and economic growth. Consequently, the US government ignored its obligation under the Bretton Woods Treaty to limit the dollar emission to the size of its gold stock, and the central bank put no brakes on the further growth of the money supply. This policy led right into a decade of inflation first and stagflation later.

The oversupply of dollars destroyed this system. The central banks in Europe and Japan became the buyers of last resort for the weakening greenback. The world experienced a massive increase in liquidity originating from the oversupply of dollars, which spilled over to the other major currencies. When the central banks in Europe and Japan bought dollars with their own currencies to stabilize the exchange rate, they expanded their domestic monetary base. After a short liquidity-driven boost, the world economy slipped into the stagflation of the 1970s.

At the same time, when Keynesianism was gaining its foothold in politics, monetarism received growing recognition in academia. According to the leading monetarist, Milton Friedman, it was not the market economy that was to blame for the Great Depression, as the Keynesians claimed, but the American central bank's monetary policy. What the Keynesians diagnosed as insufficient aggregate demand was in fact a monetary contraction.

Confronted with stagflation, the Keynesian policy knew no answer. While doing away with unemployment would require expansive policies, fighting inflation would need contracting measures. Additionally, the Keynesian policy paralyzed in the face of stagflation because high unemployment and stagnant growth meant widening budget deficits and a mounting public debt. For the Keynesians, a deflationary gap must be accompanied by a falling price level and rising unemployment. As the Keynesian theory diagnoses these phenomena as the result of a lack of demand, the government must apply expansive monetary and fiscal policies. In contrast, thus says the Keynesian doctrine, an inflationary gap results from an excess of demand which leads to inflation and over-employment. Here, the right policy is a fiscal and monetary contraction.

The principle of Keynesianism states that government expenditures should not come with a balanced government budget, but that the extra spending should happen through borrowing. With the credit-financed expenses, the state assumes budget deficits. The doctrine says the government should spend in place of the consumers and of the companies to overcome the investment weakness and the consumer restraint in the private sector. The problem with this theory is that it cannot explain why, after all, there was a falloff in investment activity in the first place.

This theory suffers from a series of fundamental problems. The model makes no clear distinction between the short and the long run as to the determinants of investments (long run) and the demand for money (short run). An insufficient distinction refers also to nominal and real variables. If the Keynesian model wants to explain unemployment, the model requires real variables. Then, however, additional government spending cannot expand the economy at will. More spending is not equal to real economic growth.

Keynesianism cannot explain the breakdown of the so-called animal spirits as the cause of the fall of investment and as the trigger to the business cycle. Extreme levels of aggregation conceal more than they reveal and a mechanistic interpretation of cause and effect between the variables makes the Keynesian model unrealistic. The Keynesian theory postulates that aggregate demand determines economic activity. Therefore, the policy recommendation says that if there is insufficient private demand, the public sector must jump in. With this theory, Keynesianism stands in contrast to classical economic theory according to which the growth of an economy depends on the production. For the classical economists, production generates the means to demand goods, as stated by "Say's law". According to the classical theory, economic crises show that technical innovations or changes in consumer preferences or the political and social environment require restructuring the economy's supply side. Keynes and his followers distort Say's law. In fact, Say's law does not say that supply creates its own demand but that for the economy in total, supply serves to exercise demand and that both variables must match. In a market economy, there cannot be an over-production and an under-consumption as the Marxists and their Keynesian followers claim. If a company produces an item that it cannot sell at the expected price, it must lower the price. When the price falls below the marginal cost of production, the company suffers losses and consequently must abandon producing this good. This happens all the time with individual companies and specific goods. If it were not so, business would be an easy game.

The Marxist term of under-consumption (because of exploitation of labor, as the theory says) signifies that the workers would produce more than they earn. Yet this claim does not hold for a competitive market economy. As long as the remuneration of a worker is below its marginal revenue product, a company will increase its overall profits by hiring more workers. A firm will stop using more workers at the point where the marginal revenue product of labor equals the wage rate. When the wage rate exceeds the revenue product of the workers, the firm must lay off labor until the two rates are equal again.

A frequently used argument says that when companies dismiss workers, the overall volume of demand will shrink and thus the slump will deepen. The answer to this claim is that if wage rates do not fall to the level of productivity, business would make losses and thus would inhibit capital accumulation. Yet capital accumulation along with technological progress must take place to lift productivity up to the wage level and to do away with unemployment. There is no other way but the dismissal of labor when the wage rate is too high because if the workers stayed in their jobs, they would provoke losses. Profits are a necessary condition of capital accumulation and a wage rate in tune with labor productivity is a necessary condition of making profits. Capital accumulation raises productivity and thereby more labor will be employed, and then the wage rate can rise.

In the perspective of classical economics, and, likewise, for Austrian economics, it is not the task of the state but that of the entrepreneurs to redirect the production structure and to adapt the production process to the altered conditions. According to the Keynesian doctrine, in contrast, the economy recovers due to government spending, which stimulates the economic actors to demand more goods and services. When this happens, so the Keynesian theory says, the economic engine will start again, and the cart will move out of the ditch. One must "crank up" the economic motor. In order to stimulate the economy, the government must apply "pump priming". At the heart of the Keynesian message, however, lies the psychological thesis that in a crisis the entrepreneurs and the consumers are too fearful to spend their money. To compensate for this, the state would have to overcome this paralysis by credit-financed extra expenditures. As demand increases, economic activity would revive because entrepreneurs and consumers would regain confidence and spend more money again.

The central problem of economic policy is complexity. In private business, complexity puts a limit on the size of companies. The larger a company, the more the data will have to be compressed to such a degree that they lose their meaning and become useless as tools of decision-making. Such aggregates as the gross domestic product and the inflation rate hide more than they reveal. That an economy shows high economic growth and a moderate inflation rate does not imply "stability". Economic growth can also result from unsustainable investment and a moderate inflation rate need not show up right away in the face of money and fiscal expansion.

It is mainly the monetary base that is under the direct control of the central bank. Although the other variables (ranging from the monetary multiplier to the long-term interest rate) are not completely autonomous, their link to central bank actions is rather loose. The monetary impulse coming from the monetary base can transform into various degrees of strength depending on the monetary multiplier and the velocity of circulation, and from there, it can affect in different degrees the components of the real economy. In turn, the performance of these components will also have feedback on the monetary multiplier and the velocity of circulation.

The expansion of the monetary base can affect both the consumer goods and the investment goods and, within the investment goods, the different stages of production. However, variations of the monetary base may likewise affect asset prices and the effect of a certain quantity of variation of the monetary base can be amplified or minimized by the monetary multiplier and by the velocity of circulation. If expansive monetary policy takes place in an environment of compensating productivity or other cost reduction gains, prices for investment and consumption goods need not rise and the excess liquidity would go into the asset markets.

Given that there are no constant quantitative relations among the variables, economic policy will be unable to calibrate their measures. One can know the direction of the impulse, in the general form that a monetary expansion tends to increase prices and that it tends to accelerate the velocity of circulation and the monetary multiplier and vice versa that a monetary contraction tends to lower the price level or put a break on its expansion while also amplifying these effects when the variables monetary multiplier and *velocity* contract. Yet both impulses become amplified, in an accelerating way with monetary expansion, and in a contractive way with a restrictive monetary stance.

It is mainly under the conditions of high productivity gains or when other factors bring down production costs on a large scale that central banks have an easy shot to achieve "price-level stability" or rather hold the inflation rate within the established target. This way, however, central banks are misled about the consequence of monetary expansion, as it does not yet show up right away in the consumer price index. By ignoring the role of the interest rate on the capital structure, monetary policy amplifies the economic expansion that began on the supply side and turns it into a demand-driven boom based on credit creation. At the end of the boom phase, productivity gains will peter out or adverse supply side shocks will occur that no longer can be easily absorbed. With the absence of compensating productivity gains, monetary impulses now feed directly into the prices of the goods. When central banks continue with monetary expansion, price inflation will result. With prices rising, the monetary multiplier and the velocity of circulation tend to increase and drive furthermore the price level upward. When instead central banks try to counter the higher price level, a contraction of the monetary multiplier and the velocity of circulation will amplify the restrictive stance of monetary policy.

Strong economic booms are characterized by high productivity gains due to new technology and often by a concurrent increase in the supply of cheap labor. By not allowing deflation to run its course under these conditions, central banks boost the boom even when they meet their inflation target. They provide ample liquidity in a situation where deflation would be required. The expansion of the money supply beyond authentic savings comes along with increasing debt levels. In such a situation, manufactured by central banks, when an excessive debt level relative to the productive base has been reached, deflation indeed becomes a problem. In a low-debt economy, the positive effects of deflation in terms of increased purchasing power outweigh its negative side and will be beneficial. In a high-debt economy, deflation becomes vicious. Therefore, the policymakers will be inclined to make the debt surge go on as far and as long as they can.

In the perspective of Austrian macroeconomics, the cure for the boom-bust cycle is the prevention of the excessive boom. However, there is little reason to expect that the policymakers would accept deflation at a stage in the sequence of the business cycle when it is possible to fabricate a boom with only moderate inflation rates.

It may be useful to remember that Irving Fisher, who was an exuberant cheerleader of the stock market boom in the 1920s, changed his intellectual course in the early 1930s when he published his "deflation theory of great depressions". Fisher's analysis (1933) saw the accumulated debt of the previous boom as the main cause for the persistence of the depression: "Thus over-investment and over-speculation are often important; but they would have far less serious results were they not conducted with borrowed money ... The same is true as to over-confidence. I fancy that over-confidence seldom does any great harm except when, as, and if, it beguiles its victims into debt" (p. 341).

7   Productivity-Led Versus Credit-Driven Booms

Money expansion comes along with new credit and represents additional spendable cash balances. This mechanism lies at the heart of Knut Wicksell's loanable fund model (Wicksell 1898). An increase in the money supply augments the supply of loanable funds beyond authentic savings. In an elementary way, "authentic savings" is that amount of loanable funds which is offered as the result of income obtained through production minus consumption. When, due to monetary expansion, the monetary interest rate falls below its natural, that is, free market, level, investors get deceived about the size of funding and embark upon credit-financed expenditures that are not matched by the availability of resources to sustain the new capital structure. In other words, the interest rate that is set below its natural level through monetary intervention deceives the economic actors about the degree of wealth of their economy and leads them to overestimate its richness. It is as if Robinson Crusoe had miscounted the amount of bananas available to him and noticed only late in his investment process that the stock of his consumption goods to feed him was too low to complete his investment project.

Keynesian macroeconomic modeling ignores this aspect. Keynesians believe that a monetary expansion augments aggregate demand and thereby national income. In real terms, however, the supply side conditions of the economy represent a production possibilities frontier to debt-driven demand expansion. A monetary expansion comes with higher expenditures, but without a corresponding expansion of the supply side, this policy results in price inflation when more effective demand chases a limited amount of goods. The capacity of the economy to produce goods and services has a limit, which is given by the availability of the factors of production. A monetary expansion will increase aggregate expenditures, but it cannot augment at the same pace the availability of resources. Albeit the more advanced macroeconomic approaches recognize the constraint that money does not foster higher production capacity, the thesis that higher economic growth could be obtained by expanding the money supply (i.e., creating demand) nevertheless continues to have prominent adherents in the profession.

The aggregate supply and demand model is mainly used in standard mainstream macroeconomics to demonstrate the impact of negative supply shocks and the futility of demand side policies as effective countermeasures. A negative supply side shock would constrain aggregate supply and provoke economic contraction and a higher inflation rate. A stagflation of this kind cannot be effectively overcome by demand measures. When capacity utilization approaches full capacity, a further demand expansion would not result in higher real growth, but only in more inflation. However, it is rarely discussed in modern macroeconomics what will happen when "positive supply shocks" occur. When, for example, concentrated technological progress occurs and/or when cheaper labor supply enters the market, the production possibility frontier[1] would expand, and in the context of the aggregate demand and supply framework such a shift

---

[1] Most of the standard macroeconomic textbook presentations of the aggregate supply and demand model make a problematic distinction between the "short run" and the "long run" or even use "medium" run (Olivier Blanchard. The Medium Run. MIT 2016) with the aim of putting the "long run" to the study of economic growth. This ambiguity is avoided when the aggregate supply curve is simply interpreted as the production possibilities frontier (Garrison. Time and Money. 2006). In a graphical aggregate supply and demand model, the production frontier curve would be vertical. As to its micro-foundation, for some authors (such as Baumol and Blinder 1997, pp. 628–642) the supply curve reflects the marginal cost

would result in a lower price level, that is, price deflation as its natural consequence.

A deflation of this kind does not imply a recession: a higher real output is now available at lower prices. The economy has become richer due to a rising purchasing power. When left to its own, the deflationary impact would be short-lived, and the economy would move smoothly to a situation where aggregate demand through new investment and more consumption would rise. This was basically what happened in capitalist economies before the inception of modern active central banking. Before central banks became active in monetary policy, recessions were short-lived, and recoveries happened accompanied by a relatively stable price level (known as the Juglar cycle). Ups and downs in business activity occurred, but these moderate swings were correctly labeled as "business fluctuations".

Before the inception of active central banking with fiat monies as their tool and fractional reserve banking in full bloom, the constraints on the money supply held back the boom and forced the economy on a path to gradual adaptation. There was no space for making the economic subjects think that scarcity had disappeared. The limited access to loans made the entrepreneurs and consumers largely rely on generated profits and forced the consumers to live within their means. Loanable funds came from the savings out of income, and thus the additional resources for investment were set free by savers who gave up on higher consumption for some time. Business fluctuations happened, but after the spurt of inventions or increasing labor supply, wages and profits became normalized when money wages would rise, and the boost of technological progress would peter out and continue at a slower pace for the next period until a new wave would appear.[2]

Without central bank intervention, the companies that benefit from the new technology or other advancements of productivity will produce more efficiently and thereby generate the funds to increase investment and provide the basis for higher income from which higher authentic savings can

---

curve, and for other authors (such as Mankiw/Reis 2010), the supply curve is purely of a macroeconomic nature and reflects expectations concerning prices and wages.

[2] "The international gold standard at the beginning of the twentieth century operated smoothly to facilitate trade, payments, and capital movements ... The world price level may have been subject to long-term trends but annual inflation or deflation rates were low, tended to cancel out, and preserve the value of money in the long run. The system gave the world a high degree of monetary integration and stability" (Mundell 2000, p. 328).

be obtained. The whiff of deflation dampens the boom, but it also provides the conditions that the following expansion can be achieved without extra credit expansion. The natural rate of interest is not artificially lowered by central bank intervention, and the economic expansion is led by productivity gains and funded by authentic savings in the basic sense that production comes first and consumption later and that immediate consumption is less than production.

This process stands in contrast to a credit-driven boom. In this case, the increase of loanable funds is provided by fiat monetary expansion and thus lacks the support of savings that come out of the income obtained through production. With the interest rate artificially low, the competitive situation forces businesses to temporarily expand production beyond the point given by the natural production level as it is determined by the natural interest rate. Without credit expansion, demand follows supply; under the condition of monetary expansion, supply is forced to catch up with the higher monetary demand that comes from credit injection. The natural path of the expansion is thus transformed into an artificial economic boom.

With the inception of active central banking, the natural process of adaptation has undergone a profound change. In contrast to the situation of passive central banking or the absence of a central bank (White 1993), modern active central banking follows the aim of making the money supply more elastic in order, as it is claimed, to "stabilize" the economy. Consequently, an inflationary bias has characterized modern central banking since its inception in the early twentieth century. The inflation-bias of modern central banks lays the groundwork for the occurrence of extended boom and bust cycles. Under the absence of substantial technological progress or other effects that expand production possibilities, modern central banks produce price inflation right away—as has been the case with the run-up to stagflation in the 1960s and 1970s. In periods of clustered technological progress, as it occurred in the 1920s and in the 1990s, low price inflation rates materialized despite massive monetary expansion. Such credit-driven booms with productivity gains at their bases do not necessarily entail higher consumer prices. Different from stagflation whose roots are more readily discernible, the "inflation-stable" boom-bust cycle remains largely unrecognized in the theoretical and statistical framework used by modern central banks. Monetary authorities usually only wake up until the cycle has gone beyond the boom phase and the economy has already progressed into the bust phase.

Modern central banking since it was institutionalized as fiat money management tends to transform a productivity-led economic expansion into a credit-driven boom that is unsustainable. Apparently assured by the fact that there is no excessive inflationary risk, monetary authorities apply expansive measures and thereby fabricate a monetary interest rate below its natural free market level. This policy moves the economy to higher debt levels. Productivity gains make it possible that credit expansion comes without price inflation as measured by the consumer price index.

By not letting price deflation occur as the natural consequence of productivity gains and other cost reductions, central banks transform an economic expansion that began on the supply side into a demand-led and credit-driven boom. Given that the period of highly concentrated technological progress occurs in time spans covering often many years, this process of monetary expansion in the face of potential deflation tends to be repeated several times. Each time when the central bank authorities fear deflationary potential, they will be inclined to augment the money supply, thereby pushing the economy to higher debt levels. A period like this will be characterized by high economic growth rates combined with low inflation rates as long as the productivity advances continue at a high pace and when no adverse supply-side shocks occur.

Credit expansion implies the built-up of an overhang of liquidity. In the boom phase most of the excessive liquidity tends to be absorbed by the asset markets, and it is no surprise that the end of the boom phase typically coincides with a stock market crash. When central banks continue to expand the money supply even when the productivity increases begin to peter out and even more so when hectic policy interventions provoke "regime uncertainty" (Higgs 1997), excess liquidity will build up higher reserve positions in the banking sector and thus paralyze active monetary policy. Different from the boom phase, when it was an easy game for central bankers to "push" the economy, monetary policy instruments became blunt in the contraction phase. However, if central banks should succeed in stimulating effective demand, price inflation will be the inevitable consequence. The constraints set by the production capacity, which may shrink due to the need of having to rearrange the existing production structure as it is provoked by the bust, will limit the effect of so-called expansive monetary and fiscal policies. In the face of a limited or shrinking production capacity, "deficit spending" by government or the private sector based on debt and not on production will produce price inflation.

Toward the end stage of the stagflation, monetary policy transmits directly into the price level.

When inflation begins to accelerate, the velocity of money circulation will also tend to increase and thereby amplifies the expansive monetary impulses. When the bust sets in, the velocity of money circulation will contract. It was this phenomenon of a collapsing money supply that attracted the attention of the monetarists. The basic error of monetary policy, however, is not the inactivity of central banks in the slump but the active stance at the inception of the boom when central banks decrease the monetary interest rates and feel vindicated by an apparently stable price level. Deceived by an apparent absence of a direct link between monetary expansion and the consumer price level under the condition of productivity gains, this relationship revives in the second stage, while in the contraction phase, the link breaks down again. The monetarist view is based on the equation of exchange and holds that the monetary aggregate multiplied by its velocity of circulation is identical to nominal national income that in turn can be split into the price component and real production. Assuming that real economic growth is determined by non-monetary factors and that the velocity of money is constant, the relationship between the monetary means of payment and the price level becomes stand in proportional relation to each other. In the monetarist perspective, there is a direct link from the variations of the monetary aggregate to the price level.

As Garrison (2005) explained, the monetarist model, however, suffers even more from over-aggregation than the Keynesian model, which at least makes a difference between consumption goods, investment goods, and government spending as well as exports and imports. Disaggregation of the variables of the demand determinants of national income reveals that national income changes through either the nominal part or the real part of aggregates or their combination because spending is the result of the multiplication of the number of goods by their respective prices. Spending ten monetary units, for example, can be the result of two goods with each a price of five monetary units or of five goods with each having a price of two monetary units. Overall spending changes as the result of the combination of goods and prices. Thus, an increase in national spending may result from an increase either in goods or in prices or in any variation of their combination.

The expansion of the monetary base can affect both the consumer goods and the investment goods, and within the faction of investment goods, it will affect investment goods across the different stages of production. Variations of the monetary base may likewise affect asset prices or exports, imports, and foreign debt, and the effect of a certain quantity of variation of the monetary base can be amplified or minimized by the monetary multiplier and by the velocity of circulation. If expansive monetary policy takes place in an environment of compensating productivity or other cost reductions, prices for investment and consumption goods need not rise and the excess liquidity would go into the asset markets. If this is the case, the monetary policy of inflation targeting is being deceived because the excess of money creation is not immediately reflected in the price level. The variations of the lags of monetary policy, which Milton Friedman (1961) already found to exist under regular conditions, expand even more when the effect of productivity is considered.

A monetary impulse coming from the monetary base can be amplified or nullified depending on the size of the monetary multiplier and the velocity of circulation. Even when assuming the rare case of a smooth transmission of the monetary impulses, the question arises as to what degree the different variables react to the cause of the monetary impulse. A variation of the monetary base may go into the prices of commodities, or it may affect mainly the prices of investment goods, or the excess liquidity may go into the asset markets or affect the external sector. When the main impulse goes to the investment goods, it will affect differently the various stages of production. One cannot determine ex ante how the impulse transmits from prices to quantities. In addition, there is also feedback at work among the different types of transaction. The original impulse affects the economic exchange differently under different circumstances, and thus there will be distinctive feedback loops on the monetary multiplier and the velocity of circulation. The velocity of circulation, for example, may remain stable over a long time, but when structural changes in the economy occur, or when new kinds of expectations take hold, the velocity of circulation will change. It is a matter of human action how much of the ones assets one will hold in cash and how ready a person is to spend. Nevertheless, there is a general tendency for the velocity of circulation to increase with the degree of inflationary expectation, and when expectations of deflation dominate, cash holdings will rise, and the velocity of circulation will tend to contract. At advanced stages of inflation and deflation, when expectations about the trend become more manifest, the feedback loop becomes even more pronounced and re-enforces the link between the general price trend, expectation and velocity leading to the extremes of hyperinflation and deflationary collapse. There are no mechanical stable relationships between the variables because they do not act by themselves but are expressions of the underlying human action. It is typical for conventional economic and econometric modeling that the models work quite well under calm conditions but break down drastically when turbulences occur. While forecasts are possible when the conditions are stable, there is no need for them, but when they would be needed because of changes in the economy, they do not work. The result is a deception of the potency of monetary policy and economic policy in general. Under smooth conditions, the confidence in the models grows and the belief rises that reliable forecasts could be made. Yet when a crisis happens, these models break down and the authorities apply wrong measures because they derive their rationale from a situation when the economy was in a stable condition.

Given that there are no constant quantitative relations among the variables, central banks are unable to calibrate their policies. One may know the direction of the impulse only in a general way that, for example, a monetary expansion tends to increase the price level. One knows that both—the banking multiplier and the velocity of circulation—amplify the money in circulation, but one cannot be certain when the effect will set in and how large their dimensions will be because of a change in the monetary base. All one knows is that there exists a general tendency that the original impulse will be amplified—in an accelerating way with monetary expansion and in a contractive way with a restrictive monetary stance. No amount of empirical research can solve this issue because the present economy will always be different from the past and in times of crisis the present economy and its future path will be radically different from the past.

Thus, the contribution of Austrian macroeconomics to monetary policy is a stark warning about the exuberance of central banking to steer the economy. When the sea is calm and all runs smoothly, forecasts are not needed, but when the storm comes up, the models no longer work.

CHAPTER 4

Bringing Capital Back into Macroeconomics

Abstract Conventional macroeconomics neglects severely the importance of capital. It is relegated to the theory of economic growth and there it gets treated as a homogeneous blob denoted as K for capital. In contrast, capital and entrepreneurship are fundamental to Austrian macroeconomics. In this theory, capital is conceptualized as a subjective phenomenon that gains its livelihood by the human action of the entrepreneur. His investment decision must deal with the problem of time and uncertainty when he embarks upon roundabout production. The accumulation of capital is contingent on savings and as such relates to time preference and the interest rate. By differentiating the micro- from the macro-aspect of malinvestment, capital and entrepreneurship come into play to explain the occurrence of economic downturns and persistent stagnations.

Keywords Capital • Time preference • Interest rate • Roundabout production • Productivity • Malinvestment

© The Author(s), under exclusive license to Springer Nature   59
Switzerland AG 2024
A. P. Mueller, *A Primer on Austrian Macroeconomics*,
Palgrave Studies in Austrian Economics,
https://doi.org/10.1007/978-3-031-75189-9_4

1   Capital and Money

Modern macroeconomics took shape in the 1990s (Taylor 1997) with the formalization of the expectations-augmented Phillips curve implying that there is no trade-off between inflation and unemployment in the long run and of a model of monetary policy which regards central bank actions in terms of rules and reaction functions with the short-term nominal interest rates as the principal instrument of monetary policy.

In contrast to the dominant schools of macroeconomic policy, Austrian scholars have consistently warned about the consequences of excessive credit growth and a monetary policy that manipulates the monetary rate of interest as an interventionist tool. In the perspective of the Austrian school, the attainment of macroeconomic policy objectives such as economic growth, high employment, and a "stable" price level do not guarantee that the state of the economy is sound. Excesses of the business cycle may well be at work even when statistical measurements should show that the price level is stable or the official inflation rate stays within a pre-set range. Indicators such as the price index, the growth rate of the gross domestic product, and the unemployment rate do not capture the underlying deeper economic forces as they take place at the level of the structure of production. Even when economic statistics show that the economy is growing, employment is high, and the price level is "stable", massive distortions may take place that transform the economy's production structure. Conventional economic indicators are mainly statistics that were developed to monitor magnitudes that are relevant in the context of models such as the Keynesian Cross, the macroeconomic equilibrium model ISLM, and the aggregate supply and demand (ASAD) models. By concentrating on these indicators as the guideline of economic policymaking, the authorities are automatically led to perceive the economic process through the lenses of these outdated models.

Even when supplemented by the DSGE model, policymakers do not recognize that even when macroeconomic data do not signal alarm but suggest the existence of a Goldilocks Economy that is neither too hot nor too cold, but warm enough with steady economic growth yet not so hot as to push the economy into an inflationary status, distortions will build up. Even without price inflation showing up, expansive monetary policy will impact the macroeconomic coordination process when the monetary authorities set the policy interest rate below its "natural" or free market level. It is only when the crisis begins that malinvestments will become visible. Then, the indicators flash an alarm. Yet it is too late for economic policy to react because economic growth is already falling, unemployment rising, and the economy is about to veer off into either deflation or inflation.

Uneasiness with conventional macroeconomics has been rampant for quite some time. The financial crisis of 2008 only highlighted once again the frustration with the state of macroeconomic theory. The ambiguities of the ISLM model have already plagued its originator (Hicks 1980/81) and its extension to the aggregate supply and demand (ASAD) model has not removed the inconsistency of the standard model (Colander 1995). Despite the deficiencies of the ISLM-AS model, it continues to serve as the main workhorse of macroeconomic analysis both inside and outside of academia. The reason is mainly the lack of an alternative model. The ISLM-AS model continues to live by default. The need is widely felt to gain a model that is simple enough for the classroom, yet also sufficiently sophisticated for advanced studies and empirical investigation.

Austrian macroeconomics provides a vehicle that applies a sharp distinction between monetary and real variables and avoids the vagueness as to the real and nominal effects that come with the concepts of "spending" or "aggregate demand". Capital-based Austrian macroeconomics goes beyond monetarism in its use of the equation of exchange. The main function of this macroeconomic model is to show the links among the main parts of the economy.

Based on the Mises-Hayek business cycle theory (Mises 1912; Hayek 1931, 1941) as elaborated by Garrison (2001), the goods side-monetary side analysis serves as a complement to the modern versions of capital-based macroeconomics. Garrison (2001), Selgin (1994) and others developed models that study the role of credit expansion in the business cycle and the role of deflation. Garrison has advanced the Austrian theory of the business cycle by developing an approach that links features of standard macroeconomic modeling with Hayek's theory of the business cycle. These models concentrate on the intermediate period and on the analysis of the production structure in the upswing and downswing phases of the business cycle. Austrian macroeconomics puts active monetary policy at the center of the analysis. It elaborates on the sequence that takes place when central banks aim at price level stability in a constellation when productivity gains would require temporary deflation.

Almost any of the common standard macroeconomic textbooks typically perplexes its students with a confusing array of poorly differentiated concepts, particularly those pertaining to capital and money. Different from this practice, Austrian economics in the Misesian tradition makes strict distinctions between money, capital goods in the production process, and capital as an accounting concept. In this classification, neither money nor financial assets are "capital". First of all, a sharp distinction needs to be made between productive capital and "capital" as an accounting concept. Productive capital refers to the arrangements of heterogeneous capital goods in the production process while accounting capital is the monetary representation of the market value of the capital goods. As to productive capital, its structure is at least as important as its size. Both the accumulation of capital *and* the unending transformation of the production process are the keys to future prosperity. Along with the distinction between productive and accounting capital and the recognition of the heterogeneity of productive capital, Austrian economics includes a further element in its theory of capital that is different from other schools: the integration of entrepreneurial appraisal. This way the Austrian theory of capital discusses money and capital in the perspective of human action which implies time, purpose, and means (Lewin et al. 2019).

The heterogeneity of capital has also an important implication for the role of money. In the Austrian perspective, money is not only an entity that impacts the price level, but it is also a ubiquitous economic factor that impacts relative prices and thereby the capital structure. Therefore, monetary policy, in so far as it determines at least to a certain degree the money supply and sets the policy rates of interest, will also affect the longitudinal structure of capital. Money expansion comes along with new credit and represents additional expendable cash balances. An increase in the money supply will augment the supply of loanable funds beyond authentic savings, and *ceteris paribus*, the monetary interest rate will fall below its natural level. With more money supplied to the market beyond authentic saving, the loan-takers are deceived about the sustainable size of funding and initiate credit-financed expenditures that are not matched by the availability of resources that would be needed to maintain an extended capital structure.

Without active central banking oriented toward specific monetary goals and fiat monies as their tool, and without a fractional reserve banking system, the constraints on the money supply would hold back the boom and thus bring the economy on a path to gradual adaptation. There would be no space for making economic actors think that scarcity had disappeared. The limited availability of credit would make the entrepreneur rely on generated profits, and it would force the consumer to live within his means. Loanable funds would come from the savings out of income, and thus the additional resources for investment would only be set free when savers gave up on higher consumption for some time. Without central bank intervention, the natural rate of interest is not artificially changed by central bank intervention, and the economic expansion is led by productivity gains and funded by authentic savings.

In a credit-driven boom, however, the increase of loanable funds by way of the monetary expansion is not congruent with savings out of income. With the interest rate artificially lowered, the competitive situation forces businesses to expand production. Without credit expansion, the sequence is that demand follows supply; under the condition of monetary expansion, the sequence is reversed: supply is forced to catch up with the higher nominal demand that comes from the credit injection. The natural path of the expansion will be transformed into an economic boom.

2   Capital and Its Use and Purpose

The productivity theory of capital dominates the popular view and public discussions. It presumes that capital generates the yield like a tree begets its fruits. In this view, more saving implies more investment and more investment generates a higher capital stock, which in turn raises future yields. The belief is widespread that monetary assets grow and render automatically the returns. Yet already at the end of the nineteenth century, the Austrian economist von Eugen von Böhm-Bawerk exploded the productivity theory of capital. He showed that without entrepreneurial action, capital is stale and useless.

There is no escape from permanent efforts to rearrange the production process. Without entrepreneurial activity, capital is just a heap of capital goods. Without the entrepreneur, capital is dead. It takes managerial activity to bring capital to life and to keep capital alive. The future levels depend on the overall conditions of the economy as they evolve over time. The need for constant renewal of real capital requires a flow of funds to maintain the production process. Financial assets will appreciate in tune with profits and thus depend on able entrepreneurs. Saving and investment will be wasteful when managers who lack foresight and prudence run the business or when institutional settings emerge that hamper, transform, and destroy these entrepreneurial qualities.

Only as an accounting tool—as "monetary capital"—can one aggregate capital and determine the change in its size. As an accounting tool, capital is the monetary representation of real capital goods in the process of production. Capital in its concrete existence as capital goods does not grow by itself or could be stored over time. One can save money, but one cannot store capital goods without loss. Capital goods left by themselves decay and during the production process they deteriorate and disappear from the process of production. Monetary capital does not generate the output which renders profits and interest. Capital renders a yield when profit-seeking entrepreneurs remodel the structure of production to changing conditions as they employ labor and find and use new production techniques.

This insight has important implications for the pension system. It says that the individual member of a generational cohort may improve his future wealth position in relation to the average by saving more, but that the conditions of the economy in the future will determine the general level of well-being. Even more so, the theory of Eugen von Böhm-Bawerk (1890) explains that savings will not contribute to the general level of the future well-being when the individuals of a cohort invest in government bonds as a form of "savings". The public deficit cancels out the net savings of the private investor and the overall amount of national savings remains unchanged. Only those savings can count as an investment which go into the hands of the entrepreneur who uses them to maintain, enlarge, and rearrange the economy's capital structure (Lachmann 1956), in the search for profits.

The stock market is not a wealth-generation machine. Expecting that financial investments now would guarantee a yield in later times is an illusory belief (Lewin 2021). Likewise, more social security contributions now do not assure higher pensions later. Lending more money to the government or paying higher contributions does not increase the capital stock. Governments spend most of the money on salaries and other items that are consumed. By saving through government bonds, there is little difference between the pension scheme of pay-as-you-go and a capital-based system. In both cases, the savings of one group is consumption by another one, and no real capital formation takes place.

The accumulation of financial assets may be an investment in the personal perspective, but it does not mean that real capital comes into existence. Investing in stocks does not automatically create more real capital. Most of the stock trade is a rotation of ownership. Higher stock market valuations appear as real wealth creation, but it is not the price of an asset that means wealth but the profits that come from the process of production. What counts for the level of wealth in the time to come is the future stream of income that results from the profit-generating entrepreneurial activity. Monetary saving is not necessarily an investment, and investment is not automatically capital formation.

From these considerations, it follows that the way to save for the future is to preserve entrepreneurial capitalism. For a nation to become wealthy, its savings must get into the hands of able entrepreneurs. To continue wealth creation and prosperity, entrepreneurs must rearrange the capital structure. Savings are the inflow to this process. Savings do not turn into lucrative investments by themselves, but to generate profits and lay the basis for prosperity, the economy needs entrepreneurs with foresight who dedicate themselves to reshaping the structure of production in the search of profits.

Higher productivity now does not guarantee that it will continue this way in the future. To preserve and improve capital, one needs incessant entrepreneurial management. Capital maintenance and its accumulation need both: perpetual savings and investment as well as the continuous rearrangements of the capital structure under entrepreneurial guidance. The economic decline of a country comes with the decay of its entrepreneurial class as, likewise, the rise of a nation results from the competence and creativity of its entrepreneurs.

Under a socialist economic system, savings and investment come necessarily along with capital destruction. But in capitalist countries, too, savings, investment, and economic growth can deceive as indicators of the performance of an economy. If it were nothing more than aggregate investment that mattered, economic development and swift wealth creation would be easy. Poor economies could become rich in a short time by borrowing abroad; and rich economies, where savings are available, could choose their desired future wealth levels.

Economic growth requires more than saving and investment, and even together with technological progress, these conditions are not enough. Only when the savings get into the hands of companies that adapt to market conditions will investment contribute to future prosperity. The entrepreneurial quality of the management and the overall socioeconomic conditions determine whether the savings are put to proper use or squandered. Economic development is only in part a matter of savings and investment. These are necessary conditions. What counts is the entrepreneurial capacity.

All present consumption comes from current production. One cannot pre-produce the goods in advance that one needs in a more distant future. The provision for consumption is a continuous process. Because the future demand will differ from today's, the capital structure which is now in existence will not be adequate in later times. Only constant adaptation and new capital formation can make sure that the production process will provide the flow of consumption goods in the periods to come. To accomplish this is the genuine task of the entrepreneur.

3   Two Concepts of Capital

Although capital and entrepreneurship play an essential—maybe *the* essential—part in the everyday workings of the modern economy, the role of capital and entrepreneurship are almost entirely absent in the mainstream version of modern macroeconomics. It is only in Austrian macroeconomics that capital and entrepreneurship play such a prominent role. The concept of the "capital structure" in terms of the stages of production has provided the foundation for the formulation of the Austrian theory of the business cycle which continues to be a major topic in the Austrian research program. A subjectivist concept of capital and a microeconomic view of the stages of production are essential to shed light on the role of profit and loss, investment, savings, and the emergence of malinvestment.

In his *Pure Theory of Capital* (1941), Friedrich v. Hayek made decisive steps forward to purify the concept of capital from its objectivist attributes but did not fully integrate entrepreneurship into his theory. The Austrian view of capital is different from the neoclassical concept. Capital is not the homogenous entity devoid of structure and time, but heterogeneous and intimately linked to time and entrepreneurial perception. From this major difference, all other differences between the two concepts of capital do follow. Keynesian economics has only expenditures in sight and abandoned capital theory altogether; and in monetarism the real economy and its capital structure have vanished completely. Almost any branch of economics outside of Austrian economics defines net investment as the simple addition to capital through gross investment minus the depreciation of the existing capital stock. This approach also presumes the existence of a macroeconomic production function whose mathematical form includes the production elasticities of labor and capital as the relationship between the input factors capital and labor in addition to a term for total factor productivity as the determinants of the final aggregate output and aggregate income.

In standard neoclassical macroeconomics, the capital stock expands or shrinks according to the difference between savings and depreciation. With savings proportional to national income at a definite rate and capital subject to a constant rate of depreciation, the economy moves to a so-called steady state, where new investment is equal to depreciation. New capital formation renders less income because production is subject to diminishing returns. For economic growth to continue when this state is reached, technological progress must come into play that enhances productivity.

In this theory, capital is stylized as a stock. Once when capital is defined this way, the replacement and maintenance of capital becomes a problem of addition and subtraction, which can take place discontinuously or periodically. In the perspective of the neoclassical growth model, net investment does not change the structure of production. Depending on the difference between gross savings and gross investment on the one hand, and depreciation, the capital stock either rises or falls or remains constant (when gross investment equals depreciation) without any impact on the structure of capital. This is obviously an assumption which is far removed from reality.

By assuming that capital can be expanded or shrunk without an impact on its structure, there is no need for entrepreneurship. This theory creates a mechanistic automaton. It comes as no surprise that non-Austrian economics treats capital (if it is mentioned at all outside of growth theory) as something that is automatically given. The decision to increase or not to increase the capital stock, or which technology to apply, vanishes from the analytics and the existing capital stock could be managed by an algorithm or a government that has the authority for central planning. Such a conception, as it is inherent in the economic growth theory of conventional macroeconomics, eliminates the essential properties of capitalist production. In this kind of model, the structural aspect of capital and the role of the entrepreneur remain in the dark. It is in this context, with the concept of capital as a measurable unit—supposedly representing the aggregate of capital goods—false theses such as that the demand for capital and labor were determined by aggregate expenditure can emerge.

By neglecting capital, modern mainstream macroeconomics has lost its access to discern one of the most fundamental problems of the business cycle: the built-up of malinvestment in the excessive boom and the rebalancing (or "re-coordination") of the capital structure in the bust.

The central problem of the non-Austrian theory of capital is the assumption of a homogenous and quantifiable capital stock. Such a theory is "bound to ignore important features of reality" (Lachmann 1956, p. 6). It disregards the heterogeneity of capital and the function of the entrepreneur must remain hidden. In such a theory "investment becomes merely a question of changing the absolute quantity of this homogeneous capital stock. Its *composition* does not interest the economist whose theory of investment is bound to be somewhat fragmentary" (ibid., p. 49).

It is different from the Austrian approach. The Austrian position holds that non-permanence is the characteristic attribute of capital goods and thus the problem of continuous reproduction and restructuring of capital receives attention. In Austrian macroeconomics, it is "not the individual durability of a particular good but the time that will elapse before the final services to which it contributes will mature that is regarded as the decisive factor. That is, it is not the attributes of the individual good but its position in the overall time structure of production that is regarded as relevant" (Hayek 1931).

Concerning the choice of technology, neoclassical economics assumes that the choice about which of the many known technological methods will be employed depends on current supply and demand conditions, and the technique employed in production is supposed to be unalterably determined by the given state of technology. Likewise, in this theory, it is supposed that capital increases in the form of a lateral expansion of production, as a simple duplication of the kind of capital already in existence.

In sharp contrast to the homogeneity thesis, Austrian capital theory (Hayek 1941) stresses that additional capital is used to make changes possible in the technique of production. In the Austrian view, additional capital leads to structural changes of capital, and as such investment is not a mere addition or subtraction in relation to an existing capital stock, but a new investment will transform the original capital structure. In this view, the relative changes in the demand for consumer and production goods determine the changes in the structure of capital. Therefore, it is not aggregate demand as given by the total money expenditure that accounts for expansion. Thus, Austrian capital theory does not need to assume that expansion of production requires the existence of unemployed resources. The structural changes of capital allow for the assumption of full employment. As a major consequence of these different views emerges the distinction that in conventional macroeconomics, particularly of its Keynesian kind, the demand for investment goods and consumer goods will move in the same direction on an aggregate basis. In contrast to this approach, the demand for capital goods will occur in the opposite direction from the demand for consumer goods in the perspective of Austrian macroeconomics.

4 THE SUBJECTIVE NATURE OF CAPITAL

It is "probably no exaggeration to say", Hayek (1979) writes, "that every important advance in economic theory during the last hundred years was a further step in the consistent application of subjectivism". Once it is recognized that capital is heterogeneous, a subjectivist approach to capital and roundaboutness is warranted as the unity of the existing capital structure is no longer objectively given but will only exist in the mind of the entrepreneur in the form of a plan. Such a perspective opens the gateway for a theory of capital that acknowledges uncertainty and "makes room for the creativity and autonomy of individual choice" (O'Driscoll and Rizzo 1985, p. 1). The subjectivist perspective leads to a view of the economic process that is fundamentally different from the objectivist position. This definition of capital can do no other than postulate homogeneity and throw out uncertainty and entrepreneurship, while the subjectivist theory of capital leads to a view of capital where uncertainty, choice, and entrepreneurial action not only receive due attention but become constitutive elements of the theory of capital.

Maybe it is no exaggeration to say that almost all difficulties of conventional macroeconomics of coming to grips with economic reality have their roots in the lack of a theory of capital. One of the problems because conventional macroeconomics abhors capital is that in contrast to labor and land, it has no objective physical dimension. Capital exists in the form of heterogeneous capital goods whose unified representation exists in the mind of the entrepreneur. The creation of capital is the result of entrepreneurial plans and comes into existence with the cost of bearing uncertainty and time. Even in a highly advanced economy, where all kinds of tools are almost immediately available all the time, including the offer of new technologies not yet in use, production takes time and occurs in stages. This is obvious at the individual business level but gets ignored for the macroeconomy outside of Austrian economics. Like all human action, entrepreneurial action requires imagination and the conscientious application of time. However, ignoring time has become a trademark of modern mainstream economics. There is no such thing as an immediate production of goods; and services also require time.

Production involves roundaboutness, the formation of capital goods instead of immediate consumption. The higher the development level of an economy, the more intricate the complexity of the process of using capital goods in production. Yet irrespective of the level of economic development, the use of the productivity advantages of indirect production requires that immediate satisfaction must be postponed in the pursuit of the exploitation of a trade-off between present consumption and its higher level in the future.

In plain sight, capital appears as an ensemble of heterogeneous production goods. Yet as such they do not yet represent "capital" in its true sense. According to Austrian theory, "capital" emerges when the heterogeneous capital goods are combined as tools in the context of an entrepreneurial plan and realized as a production process. The heterogeneity of capital goods becomes only capital proper when these production goods become tools, when they receive a specific position in a production process that is ordered for the purpose to achieve economic progress and as such capital exists as intention in the human mind of the entrepreneur who directs the enterprise. "The idea of capital has no counterpart in the physical universe of tangible things. It is nowhere but in the minds of planning men".

For economic growth to happen, simple capital accumulation is not enough. If this were the case, economic growth would be a simple endeavor and a central planning committee could easily perform economic development (Braun 2024). Yet the quintessential form of capitalist production is not capital expansion per se. In order to be productive, capital expansion must be accompanied by managing the changes in the capital structure. Any new investment implies that some parts of the capital structure will become obsolete and that, as the result of roundaboutness, the productivity gains will not show up immediately but after varying time spans. It is here that the role of the entrepreneur comes into play as the agent to manage the change of the capital structure under the guidance of expected profits and losses. This view clarifies the role of "technological progress" and avoids the troubles that modern macroeconomics has with increases in productivity due to new technologies or improvements in human capital. In the Austrian view, a change in the capital structure is always an act aimed at increasing output per capita and thus implies the search for profitable changes of the capital structure. In this perspective, the concept of "technological progress" receives its proper understanding.

Capital, in contrast to labor and land, has no natural physical dimension.[1] It is only by the entrepreneurial plan that the capital structure will gain its coherence in terms of capitalist logic. Capital as a homogenous entity exists only as financial capital and thus, in its monetary representation, serves as an accounting tool. Only in its financial representation, in terms of monetary units, can one represent capital as homogenous, and as a quantity from which additions and subtractions could be made without affecting its structure. However, in the real process of production, capital exists in the form of a structured ensemble as heterogeneous capital goods, and in this form, capital has no natural unit of measurement other than entrepreneurial valuation based on vision, expectation, and the business plan. In this perspective, capital, in its form as the production process, has two very different aspects. On the one hand, the reality of laws of nature that rule production as a physical process and, on the other hand, as an imaginary concept in the form of the entrepreneurial foresight.

Different from the common use of the term, investment, too, lacks an objective criterion. In the context of managing the capital structure investment receives its relevance not just as a numerical expression of its cost but refers to the specificity of its role which it plays in the overall capital structure. There is no fixed relation between the monetary amount of investment and its result. As it is obvious at the business level, small investments in terms of their monetary expression can have huge a huge impact on the overall profitability and vice versa. Investment is not a mechanical process that could be taken over by an algorithm but will be based on speculation

---

[1] Interestingly enough, Piero Sraffa, one of the major intellectual forerunners of what is now called "post-Keynesian" economics, put the problem quite succinctly in a letter to Joan Robinson in October 1936, although even his belated recognition after what Böhm-Bawerk had already said almost 40 years earlier seems to have met deaf ears not only by Joan Robinson regarding Sraffa's reminder that "(if) one measures labor and land by heads or acres the result has a definite meaning; subject to a margin of error .... On the other hand if you measure capital in tons the result is purely and simply nonsense ... If you are not convinced, try it on someone who has not been entirely debauched by economics. Tell your gardener that the farmer has 200 acres or employs 10 men—will he not have a pretty accurate idea of the quantities of land & labour? Now tell him that he employs 500 tons of capital & he will think you are dotty—(no more so, however, than Sidgwick or Marshall)." Quoted in King (2002, p. 80/1).

in the form of entrepreneurial appraisal that refers not only to the "quantity" of investment, but also, and even more importantly, to the question of which kind of investment goods are the best to apply, a problem, which entails also that in which form technological advancement should occur. Investment requires judgment that goes beyond enlargement or reduction, because investment will have an impact on the existing capital structure. Entrepreneurship in this sense is not so much "alertness" (Kirzner 1973)—a concept, which would imply basically costless profits from discovery—or mainly technical and administrative progress (Holcombe 2003). Investment rather shows up as the pursuit of productivity gains. It appears as purposive action in the strife toward economic progress. This means that technical advances and the improvement of human capital are embedded in the act of investment itself in so far as the activity of investing is guided by the entrepreneurial intention to apply changes to the capital structure as a tool to maximize profits.

The entrepreneur is the essential link between the market signals and the capital structure. The task of the entrepreneur in Austrian capital theory is quite different from how it is modeled otherwise in economic theory where an "investment function" is said to be the relation between the interest rate and the amount of investment flow that would happen accordingly. This approach eliminates the entrepreneurial function. Such a reductionist theory provokes the caricature of the entrepreneur as a mindless automaton on the one side and an equally mindless wild animal on the other side. In such a world, no visionary roundabout production can happen. Consequently, one could do without entrepreneurship and a socialist economy of central planning would work as good as a capitalist economy. Yet this is not the case.

Investment in new equipment requires time until the results will show up. It is in this sense that plans and purposeful action are required to bring about economic advancement. As such, investment cannot be modeled as simple additions to existing capital, but attention must be given to the fact that time will be needed before the output that is expected from the investment in new equipment will show up and exceed the current level of the standard production procedures. It is the inherent characteristic of roundabout production that the *expected* result must outpace standard production and that, in this calculation, the formation of expectations and the interest rate will play a decisive role. In terms of the results that are expected ex ante, under the conditions of present information, the expected results in profitability must outpace conventional production methods by a considerable margin the wider roundaboutness has to be applied. The insight into the nature of capital has fundamental consequences for policies of economic growth and development. In this perspective, the best public policies are not governmental guidelines, public incentives, and the support of specific investment through subsidies but a governance that provides a stable overall framework with steadiness of conditions and a government policy that welcomes high profits in the private sector.

The application of new forms of new capital will be accompanied by uncertainty about the outcome of the investment. These uncertainties exceed the expectation about future demand and include changes in the overall business climate during the process of maturation until higher productivity shows up in goods production and until the profits can be realized. In an unfavorable business environment, productivity will stagnate because more roundabout production procedures will be avoided, and standard production methods tend to be maintained. The entrepreneurial plan has no other basis than the *expected* profits seen from the perspective ex ante, that is, before the results of the investment can be observed.

5   Capitalist Production

Eugen von Böhm-Bawerk's major contributions consist in the causal explanation of the interest rate, as the result of time preference and that the unique form of "capitalist production" exists in the use of roundaboutness. For Böhm-Bawerk, the specific "capitalist production" consists in roundabout production and has the advantage of greater technical productivity while its disadvantage consists in a "sacrifice of time". Instead of the immediate use of the consumer good for consumption, an extra production of capital goods takes place whose dimension will be guided by the criterion that the higher productivity obtained by roundaboutness will overcompensate the investment of time and the other opportunity costs.

In his *Positive Theory of Capital*, Böhm-Bawerk (1884) illustrates the concept of "roundaboutness" by the example of a farmer who wants to improve his access to water.[2]

Doing business consists in the realization of entrepreneurial plans by way of a trial-and-error procedure that is guided by the criterion of profitability. Entrepreneurial action consists in coming up with plans and realizing these plans in a continuous process of adaptation to constantly emerging new circumstances. Doing business consists in maintaining the stream of goods by incessant adaptation to local and temporary conditions and as such it includes the revision of plans and expectations in the face of the changing market conditions. The appraisal and re-appraisal of the changes in relative prices is only one of the guides in the process of spatial allocation, while the availability of savings is the major signal to provide orientation as to the *intertemporal* allocation of available funds.

The attention paid to capital in its relation to time and its characteristics as being the concomitant of roundaboutness lies at the heart of Austrian macroeconomics. The realistic recognition that capital is heterogeneous brings with it a fundamentally different perspective compared to the neoclassical unrealistic assumptions. Heterogeneity of capital implies that the capital structure is built up as combinations consisting of complementary elements that are arranged by entrepreneurial plans. The unifying focal point of capital is the vision of the entrepreneur who arranges the capital goods in a way that he deems appropriate to meet future demands. With

---

[2] "A peasant requires drinking water. The spring is some distance from his house. There are various ways in which he may supply his daily wants. First, he may go to the spring each time he is thirsty, and drink out of his hollowed hand. This is the most direct way; satisfaction follows immediately on exertion. But it is an inconvenient way, for our peasant has to take his way to the well as often as he is thirsty. And it is an insufficient way, for he can never collect and store any great quantity such as he requires for various other purposes. Second, he may take a log of wood, hollow it out into a kind of pail, and carry his day's supply from the spring to his cottage. The advantage is obvious, but it necessitates a roundabout way of considerable length. The man must spend, perhaps, a day in cutting out the pail; before doing so he must have felled a tree in the forest; to do this, again, he must have made an axe, and so on. But there is still a third way; instead of felling one tree he fells a number of trees, splits and hollows them, lays them end for end, and so constructs a runnel or rhone which brings a full head of water to his cottage. Here, obviously, between the expenditure of the labour and the obtaining of the water we have a very roundabout way, but, then, the result is ever so much greater. Our peasant needs no longer take his weary way from house to well with the heavy pail on his shoulder, and yet he has a constant and full supply of the freshest water at his very door."

the concept of roundaboutness and the heterogeneity of capital it is brought to light that the outcome of investment requires time and waiting and as such investment is confronted not only with risk but with uncertainty in the sense of unknown distributions of the results. In this perspective, the role of the entrepreneur comes into play as to his specific function as the anticipator of unknown future demand and prices and therefore as the preeminent economic agent whose prime specialization lies in the ordering of the capital structure under the conditions of uncertainty. The realistic postulate of the heterogeneity of capital in terms of production goods draws attention to the stages of production and the complexity of capital structures. Quite different from the modeling that investment decisions receive in modern macroeconomics in terms of functional relationships, a realistic view puts entrepreneurial activity in the context of uncertainty and contingency.

Beginning with Carl Menger (1871) and followed up by Böhm-Bawerk (1884), the heterogeneity of capital as an ordered production structure forms the starting point for the Austrian theory of capital: "… capital is the sum of heterogeneous concrete capital goods. To aggregate them, one needs a common denominator. This common denominator cannot be found in the number of capital goods … nor their length or width or volume, or weight or any other physical unit of measurement. … The only measuring rod that does not lead to contradictions … is the value [of these capital goods]" (Böhm-Bawerk, in Hennings 1997, p. 132).

Accordingly, Lachmann (1956, p. XV) asks what it is that unites capital in its concrete representation such as it shows up as "(b)eer barrels and blast furnaces, harbor installations and hotel-room furniture" other than the entrepreneurial plan and the valuations that are derived from this plan? The arrangements that take place are arrangements in terms of an order guided by a purpose. It is a process of valuation that extends from the expectations, the plan, and the vision of the future to the present. The valuation of capital is not causal but teleological and volitional, and it is grounded in human action with its basic elements of time, stages, and purpose.

Capital as an instrument of action is a means that it serves as an entrepreneurial tool. The purpose of capital is in the mind of the entrepreneur who employs capital to gain returns. In this sense capital is a "praxeological concept" (Mises 1989, p. 512), its basis is human action. The realization of this entrepreneurial plan takes time and thus all entrepreneurial action is speculative because the plan is directed toward remote results whose exact outcome is uncertain. Capital has an inescapable speculative dimension because capital formation is constantly exposed to uncertainties and contingencies. Even in a highly developed economy, where new technologies and all kinds of goods are readily available, the individual project of production involves time and the postponement of immediate use of resources for consumption.

Human well-being requires a continuous stream of consumption goods, and thus time preference poses a limit to the potential degrees of roundaboutness. The problematic nature of roundabout production lies in the uncertainty about the determination of its adequate degree in terms of time and resources. On the one hand, roundaboutness is the way to increase productivity; on the other hand, this pursuit may become overextended in the face of the necessity of having sufficient savings available for the time it takes to finalize the project. Without roundaboutness, there is no economic progress because the application of goods to produce goods is the way how technological progress happens, but if the degree of roundaboutness is too high, incompatibilities between the urgent needs for consumption goods and the capital structure to deliver this stream of consumption goods will occur (Strigl 2000, pp. 6–14).

At the micro level, the rejection of roundabout production involves the risk of losing out to the competitor and disappearing from the market, while the pursuit of higher degrees of roundaboutness is confronted with the risk of overextension relative to savings and thus facing bankruptcy. This decision about the adequate degrees of roundaboutness constitutes the essence of entrepreneurship. It is also so shocking that this fundamental problem of economic progress gets neglected by modern macroeconomics.

6   Time Preference and Interest Rate

Economics as a part of the theory of human action deals primarily with a monetary economy based on the division of labor. Direct exchange and Robinson Crusoe models may serve as theoretical points of reference, but their fictitious character must be kept in mind. By focusing on money, Austrian economics contrasts strongly in relevance when compared to other models of economics. When applying its methodological principles to money, Austrian economics regards a phenomenon such as the interest rate or the demand for money as the result of human valuation. The central focus of the Austrian theory of money is directed at the theory of interest, as it reflects most clearly the aspect of subjective valuation.

In its primary form, the interest rate is the discount that human action must give to later available goods compared to earlier available goods, which may render the same service. Otherwise, man would not act. Human action implies by necessity a preference for the immediate. To put it in another way, in an imaginary world where it would be certain that the world would end tomorrow, time preference would become infinite and with it the interest rate because under such an expectation no one would be willing to save. The difference between the original rate and the monetary rate of interest also shows up when one imagines the full elimination of interest income (by expropriation or taxation). Then, saving would stop and provoke the consumption of accumulated capital, precisely because the primary rate of interest cannot be removed from human valuation.

The central thesis of Mises' monetary theory consists in the proposition that the monetary rate of interest may deviate from the natural rate due to money creation (or its contraction) in the credit markets. If the monetary interest rate falls below its natural level and thus deviates from the primary rate of interest, the monetary rate will deviate from the original valuation between present and future goods, and as future goods have become relatively cheaper, the demand for them increases.

By using sequential analysis instead of the fiction of an immediate or "all at once-adaptation", Mises' theory points out that money affects economic agents heterogeneously. Money cannot be neutral because it enters the economy not at once nor at the same time, nor in the same quantities for all economic agents. While money may or may not change the price level, it always will change relative prices and with it the relative fortunes of individual economic agents. In the words of Mises:

> The essence of monetary theory is the cognition that cash-induced changes in the money relation affect the various prices, wage rates, and interest rates neither at the same time nor to the same extent. If this unevenness were absent, money would be neutral; changes in the money relation would not affect the structure of business, the size and direction of production in the various branches of industry, consumption, and the wealth and income of the various strata of the population.

The monetary rate of interest cannot be neutral in the sense that it would be the monetary expression of the original rate of interest, because changes in money affect prices not homogeneously and instantly. Money enters the economy at specific points of entry and gets into the hands of specific recipients first and from there on affects the rest of the economic actors in different ways. Even if the change in the quantity of money could be known in time, and if it were known for which kind of activities it enters the economy, it is impossible to know ex ante how this will affect the different prices. It is principally impossible to foresee how, when, and to what degree individual valuations will change. Only perfect foresight could transform the monetary rate of interest into a neutral rate by applying a price premium. But the formation of expectations about a certain direction of prices is disparate and must remain uncertain.

This monetary theory based on individual valuation and sequential analysis leads to the Austrian theory of the business cycle, which holds that credit expansion and contraction bring about deviations of the monetary rate of interest from the originary rate of interest (*Urzins*), thus transmitting false signals and leading to misallocation between the production of immediate and future goods. Easy money creates an illusion of wealth and thus instigates disruptions in the production process while consumers aspire for the acquisition of goods that rank higher in their time scale. It is typical of the boom period that goods that were regarded as "luxuries" before experience an increase in demand that exceeds the rate of the increase of income. The demand for prestigious goods can indeed serve as a useful indicator to identify the peak and trough of the business cycle. Because the real wealth of the economy cannot be increased by money, disproportionalities occur within the economy, which later require reversals brought about by a recession.

7   Roundabout Production and Productivity

Any capital enhancement requires time. In this sense, roundaboutness entails waiting and the extent to which waiting is possible for the extended production process to deliver a higher output of consumption goods depends on savings. The demand for capital is not determined by the absolute expenditure going into consumption goods but rather dependent upon the relative demand for consumption and production goods. Therefore, demand for capital does not vary directly with the demand for consumption goods, but in fact moves in opposition to it (Hayek 1931; Garrison 2001).

There is a trade-off between present consumption and capital accumulation, between changes in the rate of current consumption and the degree of roundabout production. More roundaboutness means moving along the stages of production axis to higher degree of waiting and the implementation of more stages of production that are required for the production process to deliver the rise of consumable output later.

The term "stages of production" has the basic praxeological meaning that production is not a continuous process but consists in a series of distinct steps, such as it happens likewise whether producing a sandwich, writing a book, or developing a high-tech product. Production takes place in time, but it is not chronological time per se, or the average of time that matters but "economic time", that is, time defined in terms of the arrangement of production stages. These stages require a strict sequential order. The car manufacturer cannot paint the vehicle before its chassis is available. Also, the lack of seemingly minute details in the steps of the production process can halt the whole procedure or make the final product unusable or sharply diminish its value for the client as is the case, for example, when serving an omelet without salt.

A specific production good does not have a value *per se* but receives its valuation through the entrepreneur's judgment as to the position of this specific production good within the overall time-consuming process of production. The definite position that is assigned to the assemblage of specific production goods within the chain of the stages of production is the origin of the value of this specific production good and is derived from entrepreneurial judgment about his estimated future demand for the final product. The various distinct stages of production will have different durations measured by chronological time, as it happens, for example, with the time that it takes to grow a tree as opposed to felling it or transporting the good to the store and its exposition in the showroom waiting for this product to be sold and exit from the phase of production to enter and finally disappear in through consumption. The value of production goods that are physically similar or seemingly identical attain their specific value through their position within the chain of production which in turn is the result of the entrepreneurial plan guided by the appraisal of current relative prices and the expectation as to the future price structure. For a good to go through the stages of production takes time, and these stages will have different chronological durations, but in the economic perspective each phase represents a different and distinct stage of production whose relevance comes from its position within the arrangement. Like in language, meaning is not derived from the word but from its position within the sentence, while the context is derived from the purpose of communication.

A negative change in consumption represents a decrease in consumption in relation to the existing production structure. In a growing economy such a change need not signify less consumption in absolute terms but would signify reductions in consumption potential. The stages of production are represented in relation to the point where the production process results in the output of the consumption good, that is, the final good. To accomplish more roundabout production, investment has to shift from consumption and the investments at the stages closer to consumption to investment in the earlier stages of production. Accordingly, investment that is closer to the consumption point will experience a decline of potential investment together with the reduction of potential consumption. In the free market, this process is guided by the prevailing time preferences as these are monetarily reflected in the interest rate structure.

Investment in new equipment requires waiting time until the results will show up. It is in this sense that vision and purposeful action are required to bring it about. In the Austrian view, therefore, investment cannot be modeled as simple additions to existing capital, but attention will be drawn to the fact that for some prolonged time the output that is expected from the investment in new equipment will be below the level of the standard production procedures currently in place.

Roundaboutness implies a re-shifting of the existing capital structure and as such the process will be accompanied by profound uncertainty about the outcome of the investment in terms of the future demand for consumption. It is the unexpectedness of specific circumstances when the realization of plans takes place where the managerial function comes into play. In this sense, entrepreneurial management is the adaptation to the new circumstances as they emerge here and now, as the peculiar circumstances of place and time. Management consists in the transformation of the entrepreneurial vision into reality as a trial-and-error procedure under the guidance of the result as it is measured by profit and loss. Business in this sense does not begin or end with "a project" but is a never-ending process of adaptation of existing capital structures to new circumstances and the revision of expectations and the creation of new visions.

Classical economics focused on the division of labor and therefore almost exclusively on the specialization of labor and identified labor as the main origin of productivity. Austrian macroeconomics, in contrast, identifies the creation of the capital structure as the source of increases in productivity. Indeed, capital goods are "crystallized labor", but the capital structure is the work of the entrepreneur proper. While the workman gets his pay as salary for working and the capitalist gets interest for waiting, the entrepreneur gets his reward in the form of profits. Profits depend on the degree how well the entrepreneur is able to erect a capital structure that is in tune with the prevailing consumption demands when the structure is ready to produce output. In this perspective, it is obvious that there can be no certainty about the value of the capital structure before its full realization and thus for profits to earn. By its very nature, profits are a residual category and always will be.

The capitalist process that leads to more productivity consists in a process of increasing division of capital and thereby to higher degrees of capital specialization. Increasing the division of capital implies a rising level of "structural complexity" (Lachmann 1977, p. 54). A process like that cannot be grasped by a model that presupposes that capital is homogenous.

Joseph Schumpeter (McCraw 2009) characterized the capitalist process as "creative destruction" because new methods make earlier procedures obsolete. However, the emphasis should be laid more on creativity than on destruction. It is not so much destruction that happens but creative reconstruction because many if not most of the "old" capital parts will be used to create the new structure.

8   Micro- and Macroeconomic Malinvestments

Malinvestment takes place in two forms. On the individual business level, wrong investment decisions happen when the entrepreneur misreads the potential demand for his product. This kind of failed investment can be called *microeconomic malinvestment*. Competition serves to eliminate those businesses that will commit this kind of misjudgment. Competition serves as a process of selection whereby the successful entrepreneur earns profits and can go on, while the unsuccessful entrepreneur, as determined by the market participants, suffers losses and is forced to retrench or move out of the market. In this respect, market competition works as a selection mechanism that favors successful action and eliminates the unsuccessful entrepreneurial pursuit according to the final judgment by the clients of the production chain and finally by the consumers.

A different case, however, arises with an economic recession or depression, when it is not individual business errors that are the reason for losses, but that the macroeconomic environment has misled entrepreneurial action. The resulting *macroeconomic malinvestment* has a different origin and a different phenomenology than *micro-malinvestment*. These macroeconomic malinvestments arise from a systematic falsification of the signals of time preference and of the availability of resources, when a monetary policy is being applied that translates into an interest rate that transmits erroneous information and produces misleading signals about the macroeconomic conditions, particularly about the feasibility of the degrees of roundaboutness, because the policy rate is set higher or lower than the unhampered interest rate would be.

It is appropriate to differentiate between management errors and entrepreneurial errors. Management errors are failures as the result of bad administration, while entrepreneurial errors have their origin in failed roundaboutness. Failures of miscalculation of roundaboutness can be both of a microeconomic and of a macroeconomic nature. On the individual business level, wrong investment decisions happen when the entrepreneur misreads the potential demand for his product. At the micro level, these errors are inherent to the competitive process. A typical microeconomic failure of this kind occurs when the competitor comes out ahead with a superior product or beats the lagging company in having selected the better time frame for roundabout production. The successful company beats its competitors by coming out ahead of the losing business by choosing the more effective way of roundabout production. For the losing business such a case would mean that the result may be worse than for the company that adhered to standard production because failed new roundaboutness involves higher costs than the company which operates with standard production must bear. In the long run in economic development, the higher degrees of roundaboutness will bring about productivity gains, but in the day-to-day operations, the continuation of standard production methods may be less costly and therefore superior to a roundabout production that fails to get out in time ahead of the competitors. If business decisions were simply of the kind to use ever more capital and to apply the latest technology, one could do away with entrepreneurial judgment. Yet it is exactly this specifying decision as to the kind and extension of roundaboutness where entrepreneurial appraisal comes in. This kind of error is central to the economic selection process and is essentially beneficial in its consequences for the economy.

Malinvestments of the macroeconomic kind are the result of policy changes. These may affect only certain sectors of the economy or all of the economy. Errors that affect certain sectors of the economy involve all those policy changes that come with regulation, taxation, and changes in government spending. These kinds of malinvestment will cause smaller or larger disruptions in the economy and may only bring about periods of low economic growth without a deeper depression.

Macroeconomic errors, however, lie at the heart of an economic recession or depression, when it is not individual business errors that are the reason for losses, or when not only specific sectors of the economy are affected, but when the macroeconomic environment has misled entrepreneurial action. The resulting *macroeconomic malinvestment* has a different origin and of a different phenomenology than *micro-malinvestment*. These macroeconomic malinvestments arise from a systematic falsification of the signals of time preference and of the availability of resources, when a monetary policy is being applied that translates into an interest rate that transmits erroneous information and produces misleading signals about the macroeconomic conditions, particularly about the feasibility of the degrees of roundaboutness.

While micro-malinvestment business errors tend to cancel each other out and make for an improvement of overall economic efficiency, because the mechanism of selection is also a device of learning and as such serves as a promoter of economic progress, business decisions that are misled by erroneous macro signals (mainly the manipulation of the interest rate, but also labor costs, the exchange rate, and overall relevant prices such as those for energy inputs) will result in collective entrepreneurial errors, and it is in this sense that "any business cycle theory is essentially a theory of error" (Hülsmann 1998, p. 1). Here the miscalculation of time is the result of an interest policy that has deceived entrepreneurs across the board about the availability of savings. In so far as the interest rate affects any investment decision, the overall business community is enticed to embark upon roundaboutness of a degree that will later prove to have been too far-reaching. This is the case where there is first a strong boom that only will be followed by a massive bust and in its extreme form brings about economic recession and depression. In this regard the monetary interest rate plays a central role in the entrepreneurial decision if and to what extent roundabout production will be initiated and to what extent it will result in success or failure.

It is typical for the occurrence of macroeconomic malinvestment that a monetary interest rate is brought into existence that does not reflect the availability of savings but the supply and demand for credit. In the modern monetary system, such a divergence is more the rule than the exception because it is not only by monetary policy decisions that such a deviation will be brought about, but such a divergence between the monetary interest rate and the natural rate is also inherent to the workings of a fractional reserve banking system (Huerta de Soto 2012). An interest rate that is set too low in relation to a rate which would equilibrate authentic saving and investment induces businesses to embark upon roundaboutness to a degree that is not sustainable given the availability of authentic savings, that is, that amount of savings that reflects the state of time preference.

The consequence of an additional money supply is equal to an apparent increase in savings, yet it is an increase that is not based on the prevailing rate of time preference. In such a case, entrepreneurs are enticed to embark upon the pursuit of projects that cannot be finalized because consumers are unwilling to give up part of their demand for consumption goods. The business demand for funding investment clashes with the demand for final goods by the consumers. The result of this clash will be the emergence of unfinished projects when this policy must be abandoned as the economy runs into bottlenecks or creditors begin to panic. In the bust phase "idle resources" will emerge, in the form of both unusable capital and unemployable labor. Yet it is not the existence of "idle resources" per se which constitute the problem, but the underlying causes that point to projects of failed roundaboutness for which the idle resources stand as a symptom.

Relative prices of goods and services together with the price for labor and the interest rate as the price for waiting serve as the essential tools of information as to how the entrepreneurs should arrange the production structure, and it is these signals that also provide the incentives in the ongoing process of capital structuring (and restructuring). As it is the case with other policy interventions, when the price system gets manipulated by policy or distorted institutions have emerged (as it is the case with fractional reserve banking in the context discussed here), the interest rate tends to transmit false signals and provides false incentives. A deviation of the monetary interest rate from its natural level, as it would result from the unhampered interplay between foregone consumption and investment, produces errors that show up in the structure of production. The degree of the implementation of roundaboutness must be in tune with time preference, the availability of resources in the form of authentic savings, and the purchasing power and tastes of the consumers. This coordination gets disrupted when false signals are provided by the interest rate. Fractional reserve banking falsifies both to the upside in the boom and to the downside in the bust, the availability of authentic savings. While the phase of the credit glut deceives the entrepreneurs with the illusion of an abundance of savings, the opposite happens in the phase of the credit crunch where savings in fact are available but the financial intermediaries hold back lending.

Given that all entrepreneurial activity is directed toward an unknown future, the occurrence of error is unavoidable and cannot be eliminated how elaborate or sophisticated the tools of prognosis ever should become. This condition of inescapable speculation is the root of entrepreneurial profit and loss. Speculation implies the uncertainty of success or failure. Even more so, in economic speculation, the actors do not play against machines whose "class probability" (Mises 2010) can be mathematically established, but operate in the context of a social environment of unexpected change where not only the future is unknown but current price information is incomplete and where estimates of probability are irrelevant not only because of the uniqueness of decisions (Shackle 1949) but also because of the heterogeneity of the situations (Lachmann 1977, p. 26). The closed character of non-Austrian capital theory has not only expelled the role of the entrepreneur, but with this elimination, this theory has also blocked its approach toward an adequate understanding of malinvestment and business failure.

An unfavorable business climate will discourage the undertaking of roundaboutness, and even if property rights are guaranteed, roundabout production will be discouraged when strict competition laws and excessive levels of taxation limit the realization of higher profits. It is characteristic of new production techniques that they become the standard over time, and thus the competitive advantage from innovation has a limited life span. As much as there is competition between firms regarding the best product, the other major competitive factor is the question of what kind of capital to apply. In an unfavorable business climate, investment will mainly occur in standard production and more roundabout production procedures will be avoided. Under such conditions, increases in productivity will not come about.

Outside of the Austrian economics approach, the subjective, structural, and time-consuming aspect of capital formation gets neglected and with it comes the view that it is purely quantitative additions or subtractions to an existing capital *stock* that would count. Along with this view, many other aspects also get lost such that capital formation is highly vulnerable to detrimental policy interventions. An uncertain legal environment induces business to shorten the degrees of roundaboutness or to refrain altogether from entrepreneurial activity and to become merely an administrator.

The value of production goods that are physically similar or seemingly identical attain their specific value by their position within the chain of production which in turn is the result of the entrepreneurial plan guided by the relative prices and the expectation as to the future price of the resulting consumption good. For a specific good to go through the stages of production requires time, and these stages will have different chronological durations, but in the economic perspective each phase represents a different and distinct stage of production whose relevance comes from its position within the arrangement. Like in language, meaning is not derived from the individual letter but from its position within a word, and where likewise a word derives its meaning from the context in which it stands, with all of that linked to the purpose of communication.

The concept of capital as roundaboutness based on entrepreneurial plans provides the starting point of the distinct Austrian theory of the business cycle as it emerged with the contributions of Ludwig von Mises and Friedrich von Hayek. The main contrast between the Austrian approach and other theories is that in the Austrian tradition, capital expansion and its contraction are located in the changes in the longitudinal structure of the process of production. Thus, expansions and contractions imply a restructuring of the *present* state of the capital structure. "Investment decisions determine not merely, as Keynes would have it, the 'rate of investment', but also determine the concrete character of each new capital good … Each new capital good forms part of a whole and must fit into a capital combination" (Lachmann 1977, p. 117). Thus, in the perspective of Austrian economics, industrial fluctuations are not just the result of maladjustment between planned savings and planned investment, but also the result of structural maladjustments.

The concept of the stages of production has its anchor not in the past but in the future, in the way how production process results in the output of the final good. All factors of production receive their economic remuneration by the final sale of the product (Cwik 2024). The monetary value of the final sale determines the monetary compensation of the factors of production. The natural process of economic expansion occurs due to the starting point of a lower time preference which implies an increased readiness by the economic actor of sacrificing time. More time for waiting allows a shift of resources to the more remote stages of production of the roundaboutness from where it will take more time until the final goods will be finished and paid for by the consumers. As a consequence, the production frontier will expand which sets the condition for a higher output later and consequently a higher level of consumption. In other words, roundaboutness of this kind means the recognition that before a good can be consumed, it must be produced at first, and given that time preference has decreased, a higher degree of roundaboutness becomes possible and investment movers to the earlier stages of production.

CHAPTER 5

Interrelation of the Monetary Side and the Commodity Side of the Economy

Abstract Modern textbook macroeconomics dedicates much space to the supposedly "real" side of the economy versus the "nominal" side, yet has been unable to achieve a clear separation between the two aspects. The analysis of the interaction between the monetary side and the commodity side has remained muddled. It is different from Austrian macroeconomics. Based on the analysis of the relation between capital, money, and time, Austrian macroeconomics can integrate the financial sector into its theory of the business cycle and offer an elaborate depiction of the sequences that characterize credit-driven booms and their consequent busts. On this basis, Austrian macroeconomics can derive pertinent lessons from what happened in the Great Depression and come to a set of policy implications derived from Austrian macroeconomic theory.

Keywords Mainstream macroeconomics • Financial sector • Business cycle • Production frontier • Credit-driven boom • Great Depression • Economic policy

© The Author(s), under exclusive license to Springer Nature
Switzerland AG 2024
A. P. Mueller, *A Primer on Austrian Macroeconomics*,
Palgrave Studies in Austrian Economics,
https://doi.org/10.1007/978-3-031-75189-9_5

1   STATE OF MAINSTREAM MACROECONOMICS

Only after a short time when Olivier Blanchard—a leading representative of modern macroeconomics and a former economist for the International Monetary Fund—had declared that "the state of macroeconomics is good" (Blanchard 2008), the international financial market crisis broke out and exposed modern macroeconomics as an emperor without clothes. Different from many economists who work in the tradition of Austrian economics, academics who follow the paradigm of the new macroeconomic synthesis had not only failed to give any forewarning about what was to happen, this branch of economics had also very little to contribute to the explanation of the causes and of the sudden contraction or provide a recipe of how to handle the crisis other to inject even more liquidity into the markets. Before the economic downturn took them by surprise, prominent representatives of modern macroeconomics had announced a new era called "The Great Moderation" and claimed that modern "scientific" macroeconomics had the knowledge and the tools, particularly in monetary policy, to manage the economy and keep it on a path of stable growth.

The creators and followers of the synthesis between the "new" Neo-Keynesian and the "new" neoclassical models in the form of Dynamic Stochastic General Equilibrium (DSGE) models have praised their work as the epitome of scientific achievement in economics, albeit the relevance of these models for the economic policy have remained dubious.

For policymaking, the models of modern macroeconomics are still deeply marked by the older demand-side theories according to which a higher interest rate is supposed to suppress demand and a lower interest rate to stimulate the economy. Does one really believe that central bankers consistently react to unemployment and inflation by adequately raising or lowering the interest rate and that money is "neutral" in the long run and "equilibrium" easily gets re-established after temporary shocks cause a deviation? It is no wonder that the idea of the great moderation appeared with the thesis that the economy is on a long-term growth path around which it oscillates due to shocks but will come back to its trend line due to the sophisticated actions of central bankers who hit the economy on its head when it sticks its head out above the trend and gives the economy a kick (called stimulus) on its behind when it is below its potential.

In contrast to the members of the DSGE school (see Handbook of Economic Expectations 2023), Austrian scholars have consistently warned about the consequences of excessive credit growth and a monetary policy that manipulates the monetary rate of interest as an interventionist tool with the claim that this is the way how to steer the economy on a path of expansion, avoid high unemployment, and keep the economy within the limits of moderate rates of inflation. In the perspective of the Austrian school the attainment of these macroeconomic policy objectives such as economic growth, high employment, and a "stable" price level does not guarantee that the state of the economy is sound. Austrian macroeconomics holds that the business cycle may well be at work even when statistical measurements should show that the price level is stable or inflation stays within a pre-set range. In the perspective of Austrian economics, indicators such as the price index, growth of the gross domestic product, and the unemployment rate do not capture the underlying deeper economic forces as they happen at the level of the structure of production. In other words, even when economic statistics show that the economy is growing, employment is high, and the price level is "stable", massive distortions can take place that transform the structure of production and remain largely undetected. This is the case when the attainment of the prime macroeconomic policy targets—low rates of unemployment and inflation—is the result of loose monetary policy and an interest rate that is set below its "natural" free market level. It is only when the crisis begins that malinvestments will become visible as they show up in the form of falling rates of economic growth and rising unemployment with the risk that the economy veers off into either deflation or inflation.

The main purpose of the construction of the ISLM and ASAD models was to deliver analytical tools for economic policy. The goal was less to explain how the economy works, but to propose instruments for policy-making (Mankiw 2006). Internal inconsistencies of the model, which would be injurious from the scientific point of view, mattered less than the heuristic value of the approach. The ISLM-AS model has become the standard as the analytical workhorse for the teaching of macroeconomics. In terms of its scientific merit, it has been mainly because of the lack of alternatives that this approach still enjoys its standing in the classrooms as well as in the halls of power.

Different from ISLM-AS analysis, the New Keynesian and the real business cycle approach, including "dynamic stochastic general equilibrium" (DSGE) models, have gone the other way and sacrificed realism in favor of rigor with dubious results as to their relevance (Faust 2012). The financial crisis of 2008 renewed old concerns about the explanatory potency of the established approaches to macroeconomics (Blanchard 2010). The prominent protagonist of the ISLM model (Hicks 1937) criticized its set-up and usage already much earlier because of the standard model's omissions and inconsistencies (Hicks 1980/81).

In the Keynesian-type models, for example, the move of the curve of effective demand happens *uno actu* with the responding shift of the equilibrium position to a new output as if there were no limits to production and thus as if scarcity were non-existent. In the ISLM model, business and consequently capital (Garrison 2001) are absent along with entrepreneurship (Coase 2012). Colander (1995) points out that the aggregate supply and demand (ASAD) analysis is logically incompatible with the ISLM model of aggregate demand because the Keynesian approach requires a fixed price level, while the construction of the aggregate supply and aggregate demand model explicitly employs price level changes. The ISLM and ASAD models do not differentiate strictly between real and nominal values and between the short and the long run (and what lies in between). The New Keynesian models (Romer 2000) exhibit paradoxical outcomes when the economy is at or near the zero-bound of the interest rate (Cochrane 2013). The need is widely felt to have an alternative model which could substitute or at least complement and challenge the standard model.

The ISLM-AS model addresses the difference between the "real" and the "monetary" side of the economy in a misleading form. In this model, the IS curve is to represent the "real" side of the economy, when, however, the magnitudes of aggregate demand are expenditures, that is, monetary values. Demand determines production, yet this requires a constant price level or the limitation to one period. Neither the original ISLM model nor its expanded ISLM-AS version differentiates systematically between economic expansion (more output) and economic growth (capital accumulation and technological progress).

In as much as the Keynesian macroeconomic models do not represent Keynes, modern neoclassical macroeconomics (Barro 1989) does not reflect classical macroeconomics. In the neoclassical macroeconomic theory, the very subject of macroeconomics evaporates as a subject. As a type of analysis, this approach boils down to an exercise in microeconomic techniques applied to public economic issues. Although these models are an offspring of monetarism (Friedman 1956), which put money back into macroeconomics, most versions of the rational expectations and the new classical macroeconomics have expelled the role of money from macroeconomics altogether and have become intentionally oblivious to financial markets and the monetary transmission mechanism. The DSGE models have eliminated most of the "interesting" macroeconomic questions and many of the relevant issues (Buiter 2009). They ignore financial markets (other than as "frictions") and from early on have removed money (Kregel 1985) until it has vanished almost completely (Laidler 2013).

2   Capital, Money, and Time

The attention paid to capital in its relation to time lies at the heart of Austrian macroeconomics. Based on Böhm-Bawerk's concept of capital (Böhm-Bawerk 1884) and the Mises-Hayek business cycle theory (Mises 1912; Hayek 1931, 1941), the following expositions are an extension of the modern versions of capital-based macroeconomics. Garrison (2001, 2005) and Huerta de Soto (1998, 2012) in particular have presented studies of the role of monetary policy as the promoter of the business cycle using some of the analytic tools that are common in neoclassical economics and have put the Austrian approach into the context of Keynesian, monetarist, and rational expectations theories. Garrison (2005) has advanced the Austrian theory of the business cycle by developing an approach that links standard macroeconomic modeling with the Mises-Hayek theory of the business cycle.

Modeling capital as heterogeneous represents a fundamentally different perspective compared to standard neoclassical synthetic modeling. With the concept of roundaboutness as the time required to gain higher productivity and the heterogeneity of capital, it is brought to light that the outcome of investment requires waiting, and as such investment is confronted not only with risk but with uncertainty in the sense of unknown distributions of the results. In this perspective, the role of the entrepreneur comes into play as to his specific function as the anticipator of unknown future demand and prices and therefore as the preeminent economic agent whose prime specialization lies in dealing with uncertainty. The realist postulate of the heterogeneity of capital in terms of production goods draws attention to the stages of production and the complexity of capital structures. The valuation of capital is not causal but teleological and volitional, and it is grounded in human action with its basic elements of time, stages, and purpose.

In contrast, neoclassical macroeconomics puts the capital structure in a black box called K for capital from where the output, called Q, emerges. From this the divide between micro- and macroeconomics has emerged that relegates production and cost analysis to microeconomics and elaborates the exchange features, while macroeconomics deals with the large aggregates—consumption, investment, and government expenditures—or the price level and real and nominal national income aggregates. In this respect there is little difference between the "economics of Keynes" and the hyphen-Keynesian and the new hyphen-classical economists and monetarism.

In modern macroeconomic growth theory, it is assumed that it would be possible to make a clear separation between the different factors of production as to their specific contribution to output. In this framework, it is assumed that these factors could be neatly separated and that there is no connection between capital and the human entrepreneurial mind. This approach is incapable of recognizing that the production of capital requires, first of all, an entrepreneurial idea and that production comes into existence through human action based on an idiosyncratic and an ex ante improvable view about future market conditions. In textbook macroeconomics, capital investment and depreciation are regarded as simple additions and subtractions from a given a-historical capital stock. This view amounts to more than only a specific analytical device, because it systematically excludes the structural aspect of capital. Through this convention the essential elements of capital get lost in over-abstraction and over-simplification. With the concept of capital as a homogeneous unity, the erroneous idea emerges that the demand for capital and labor would be determined by aggregate expenditure.

In the Austrian version of capital theory, the stream of goods needs incessant adaptation to local and temporary conditions—guided by the purposive human action to avoid losses and gain profit. The stabilizers of this system are the individual economic agents guided by relative prices (Hayek 1984, p. 18) as they observe (information) and heed (incentive) the signals. The interest rate is the major signal to provide orientation as to the *intertemporal* allocation of available funds. Probably the most important insight of Hayek's contribution to the Austrian theory of capital is that capital is scarce in the specific sense that there exist more opportunities (including technological options) than can be realized given the present state of funds as they come from savings. There is a basic trade-off in place between the demand for consumption goods and investment goods, that is, between consumption and savings or between lower consumption now in favor of higher consumption later and higher consumption now at the cost of consumption that could otherwise have been higher in the future.

Relative prices of goods and services together with the price for labor and the interest rate as the price for waiting serve as the essential tools of information as to how the entrepreneurs should arrange the production structure, and it is these signals that also provide the incentives in the ongoing process of capital structuring and its restructuring. As it is the case with other policy interventions, when the price system gets manipulated by policy and thereby distortions of supply and demand are brought about, monetary interventions will falsify the interest rate and produce a deviation from its natural level, as it would otherwise result from the unhampered interplay between foregone consumption—authentic savings—and investment. The production of capital goods must be in tune with intertemporal preferences, the availability of resources (authentic savings), and the tastes of the consumers. This coordination gets disrupted when false signals are provided by the policy interest rate.

3   The Role of the Financial Sector in the Boom-Bust Cycle

When price inflation begins to accelerate, the velocity of money circulation will also tend to increase, and it will amplify the original monetary impulses. Likewise, when the bust sets in, the velocity of money circulation will contract. Liquidity is a market phenomenon and as such it will increase in the boom and contract in the bust. Psychology—so-called optimism and pessimism—is only an accompanying phenomenon. It was the collapsing money supply that attracted the attention of the monetarists. The basic error of monetary policy, however, is not the inactivity of central banking in the slump, but the active stance that was taken at the inception and artificial continuation of the boom, when central banks lowered the monetary interest rates and felt justified by an apparently stable price level. Fooled by the absence of a direct link between monetary expansion and the consumer price level under the condition of productivity gains, this relationship revives in the second stage, but in the contraction phase, the link will break down. As a former central banker, Alan Blinder (1999, p. 6) admitted that the monetary policymakers in the central banks operate with an unknown model, an unknown objective social function, and therefore do not possess an optimal policy rule.

The monetarist model assumes that real economic growth is determined by non-monetary factors and that the velocity of money is trend-stable and therefore that the relationship between the monetary aggregate and the price level becomes proportional. In the monetarist perspective, there is a direct link from the variations of the monetary aggregate to the price level. To gain a better view of what is going on with the supply of money, however, it is necessary to disaggregate the quantity of money and to demonstrate effects of monetary policy. The monetary aggregate of the means of payment consists of the monetary base multiplied by the monetary multiplier. The resulting number represents nominal national income which in turn must be disaggregated into the price and goods components of consumption, investment, government, and external sector. Beyond these conventional aggregates, one should also include asset prices as they also form part of aggregate demand.

The original impulse that comes from the monetary base will affect the different transaction classes and have different degrees of feedback on the monetary multiplier and the velocity of circulation. Given that there are no reliable quantitative relations among the variables, central banks are unable to calibrate their policies. There is no certainty as to whether the monetary impulse will affect in a specific way a specific variable. Only in the most general form can it be said that an inflation of the monetary side will affect the "goods side".

Keynes (1936) identified irrational entrepreneurial decision-making as the supposed reason for economic instability, while consumption expenditure was deemed to rise and fall as a stable function of income. The decision to invest is ruled by the entrepreneur, who—in Keynes' view—is driven by an unreliable "animal spirit". Keynes paints a picture of the personality of the entrepreneur that in a paranoid way shifts between greed and fear like a maniac on the one hand but resembles also a spiritless machine on the other hand, a brainless automaton that *reacts* without anticipation or purpose to present conditions in a primitive way. Likewise in Keynesianism, there is no place for a far-sighted entrepreneur who envisions future demand and acts accordingly by applying resources to the production process in the present while anticipating demand for a consumable product in the future banking on the expectation that roundabout production will succeed. By projecting such a view upon the entrepreneur as the person who holds the decision about investment in his hand, Keynes and his followers were led to believe that a market economy is inherently unstable and therefore the fatherly (so-called rational) hand of government is required to smooth out the economic process.

It is a fact that the entrepreneurial spirit may break down. However, the reason for that is not inherent to the entrepreneur's personality, but it is the result of a series of deceptions that have come from the monetary data (along with the deterioration of the business climate as it is encapsulated in this generic term), which makes the entrepreneur act like a ping-pong ball. When the interest rate, as the monetary indicator of time preference, is manipulated in the hands of the government and by the central bank as its branch, entrepreneurial decisions lose their anchor (Herbener 2002). The political interest rate manipulations deceive the entrepreneurs about the true time preference that is prevalent in the economy. Additionally, the fractional-reserve banking system not only transmits the monetary impulses that come from the central bank but serves as their amplifier. Such an economy will be characterized by instability, volatility, and uncertainties that exceed widely the capacity to manage the uncertainties at the micro-level for the handling of which the entrepreneur and business manager are the specialists. The monetary impulses that come from the central bank and their amplification by the financial sector distort the interest rate as the central signal about time preferences and as the indicator of the availability of resources and thereby bring about distortions of the business decision.

Under the modern monetary regimes, nominal loanable funds that are available in the economy do not only come from authentic savings, but also come from monetary expansion and contraction. Given a certain monetary impulse from the central bank, the financial sector tends to amplify the expansionary impulses under an optimistic environment, while the financial sector may also abort expansive impulses and produce a credit crunch under a pessimistic business climate. Even if both the investment and the savings functions should be stable, changes in the amount of loanable funds can occur due to the swings of monetary expansion and their transmission through the financial system.

The interest rate guides the amount of investment and the degree to which extent roundabout production processes will be initiated. However, in modern economies, credit creation takes place not just for business investment, but also for consumption and investment in the asset markets. In this regard, it is not only the supply of loanable funds that is highly unstable, but credit demand, too. Along with the *supply* of funds for business investment, volatility is also produced even if the business investment *demand* for real capital is parametrically fixed. In the market for loanable funds not just the supply curve shifts, but also the demand curve will move around in the absence of changes in the business investment curve and authentic savings.

It is not difficult to imagine how business decisions get distorted through monetary policy when the supply of loanable funds is highly unstable as the result of monetary policy. When the interest rate signal has been suppressed and gets distorted due to central bank intervention, entrepreneurs receive no information about the changes in time preferences and consequently cannot adapt production stages to the rising demand for consumer goods.

4   Natural and Cyclical Production Frontiers

Economic models do not represent reality but are constructed to provide orientation and a framework of analysis. Behind every economic phenomenon and each macroeconomic magnitude lies individual human action. It is this double reference, the micro-macro relation that constitutes the macroeconomic problem *sui generis*: the coordination of individual action within a specific economic environment, particularly those conditions that are common to all economic agents, as they are given by the main means of economic communication, such as money and the interest rate as signaling devices. Although money gains existence only through individual human action, it also has a meta-structure and, in this respect, money is like language or the legal system. In a functional perspective, money serves as an essential tool for coordinating individual human actions and communicating economic issues within society.

In the aggregate supply and demand models of modern macroeconomics, the intersection of the aggregate supply and demand curve determines the price level and the size of the overall output. The capacity of the economy to produce goods and services has a limit, which is the availability of the factors of production. A monetary expansion will increase aggregate expenditures, but it cannot augment at the same pace the availability of resources. The standard aggregate demand and aggregate supply analysis demonstrates the futility of trying to produce higher economic growth by expanding the money supply beyond the frontier of the natural unemployment rate and shows how negative supply side shocks cannot be simply countered by counter-cyclical demand side policies. Given the constraint that is built into aggregate supply, demand expansion would not result in higher real growth but result in a higher price level. With a few exceptions, such as in Baumol and Blinder (1997, p. 628), who use cost and profit as the analytic foundation of the aggregate supply curve, the textbook model of aggregate supply and demand suffers from over-aggregation and is devoid of a micro foundation. A solid concept of capital is largely absent, and when a reference to capital appears, capital is usually conceptualized as homogenous. The aggregate supply and demand model is basically a Keynesian model that shows that Keynesianism does not work.

In order to demonstrate the limits of money-induced economic expansion, a different kind of model is needed. At first it will be useful to differentiate between a natural production frontier and a cyclical production frontier. The natural production frontier represents that amount of production goods at which the companies produce at an output level that exerts no pressure to increase prices or to cut back on investment and labor. The natural production frontier serves as a normative reference point in the logic of human action. In the form of an empirical generalization, business leaders possess a rule to judge whether their current business activity deviates from the normal (or natural) level. In contrast, the cyclical component—as it is given in the cyclical production possibilities frontier—would refer to a situation, where the economy is in a state of excess of use of capacity or suffers from abnormally high idle capacity.

The natural production possibilities frontier represents that level of output, which is congruent with the availability of resources as it is given by the current state of the factors of production without neither stress nor idleness. Companies are only temporarily capable of managing an output level at the maximum of the potential. Not only because of the cost structure whose exact details are hard to establish anyway, firms avoid full usage of their capital because of managerial restraints. Rather, production will oscillate around the natural level, which serves as the managerial guidepost to differentiate between overheating and slack. As it is with the stages of production, the praxeological meaning of the natural and cyclical production is an ideal type. As to the microeconomic foundation, one can refer to a supply model where the cyclical production possibilities frontier is derived from the marginal cost curve. In a microeconomic supply model of this kind, the vertical curve represents the natural state of business affairs while the cyclical production possibilities frontier shows the variation possibilities that result from a given state of the factors of production that are embedded into the company's overall investment. In this sense the production possibilities frontiers represent states of affairs where the firms work at certain output levels that are judged as natural or cyclical by the entrepreneur.

In this context, different types of economic growth (negative and positive) and economic fluctuations can be defined. Authentic economic growth would be an expansion of the productive capacity. This would show up as a shift of the natural production possibilities frontier to a higher capacity. Likewise, a loss of productive capacity reflects a lower level of potential output. These kinds of positive and negative economic growth represent changes in real terms and reflect the extent of the available factors of production. An economic expansion only in nominal terms (expansion of money supply or increase of velocity) would occur with rising demand that is not matched by real capacity. In this case the expansion will not take place as authentic economic growth but as a cyclical phenomenon. It is unstainable in the same way as one can sprint only a short time in contrast to the capability of taking a long walk. Likewise, for the economy, the production capacity (as given by the natural production frontier) does not rise because of a brief boom. Although it has become common to call such short-lived expansions also "economic growth", it is not authentic growth because it can only take place as a short-lived upswing as part of the cyclical activity. The more the economic activity gets pulled by higher demand, the more such economic expansion comes with rising prices. In the microeconomic model, the cyclical production would show up as a movement along the marginal cost curve that gets steeper the more output is moving toward the absolute production limit where all additional demand expansion would finally fully go into higher prices. Movements along the cyclical production possibilities frontier curve from below up to the natural production possibilities frontier would be an economic expansion in the form of an economic recovery, while a further movement along the cyclical production possibilities frontier beyond the natural frontier would constitute an artificial economic boom.

The so-called equation of exchange, which equals money multiplied by the velocity of transaction to nominal national income composed of real production and the price level, can be reformulated by isolating the real production in the equation. Then, the "monetary side" shows up as the product of money and its velocity of circulation divided by the price level and is equal to the "real side" represented by production.

The supply side represents the production of commodities while the "money side" represents the aggregate demand. Hayek used this distinction between the *Güterseite* (commodity side) and the *Geldseite* (monetary side) to explain that "changes in the price level coming from the 'goods side' are not only not detrimental but are even necessary if disturbances of equilibrium are to be avoided" (Hayek 1984, p. 100).

The "commodities side" represents production as it happens at the level of the firms. The money side represents demand in the form of aggregate expenditures because money constitutes a common link among *all* parts of the economy. At the macroeconomic level, demand equals total expenditures. In this respect, aggregate demand is linked to the money supply, while money supply is linked to the velocity of money circulation. Aggregate demand reflects changes on the *monetary* side of the equation of exchange, while the natural production possibilities frontier shifts as the result of changes in the availability of the factors of production and their productivity. Given a fixed money supply, an expansion of productive capacity would ceteris paribus result in higher real wages due to falling prices and an increase of the purchasing power in the economy. The cyclical production, however, would play no major role in the performance of the economy in the long run as it is nothing more than what once was called business fluctuations.

Without active central banking oriented toward specific monetary goals and fiat monies as their tool, and without a fractional reserve banking system, the constraints on the money supply would hold back an excessive boom and thus bring the economy back on its path in line with its long-term economic growth potential that is determined by the size and productivity of the factors of production. There would be no space for making economic actors believe that scarcity had disappeared. The limited availability of credit would make the entrepreneur rely on generated profits, and it would force consumers to live within their means. Loanable funds would come from the savings out of income which in turn would be linked to production, and thus the additional resources for investment would only be set free when savers gave up on potential consumption and save. Without central bank intervention, the natural rate of interest changes only internally, consistent with the time preference. Thus, the economic expansion is sustainable because it is led by productivity gains and funded by authentic savings. In a credit-driven boom, however, where the boom results from the interest rate policy of the central bank, the increase of loanable funds is not brought about in a natural way but provided by the monetary expansion, and as such it is not congruent with savings out of income. With the interest rate artificially lower than under purely free market conditions, businesses cannot refrain from expanding their production even if they should recognize that it is fake. Competition forces individual businesses to take place in the run and make use of cheap money and invest to expand their production and make the production process more productive. Firms cannot simply opt out and renounce new credit that is offered at these low interest rates. The competitive situation forces the individual business to invest in the new technology when it becomes financially obtainable. The interest rate works like any other price. In the same way that businesses will increase or reduce production when prices are raised or lowered by interventions in the goods markets, they must react also to the interest rate be it above or below the natural market equilibrium. Without credit expansion, demand would follow supply; under the condition of monetary expansion, supply is forced to catch up with the higher nominal demand that comes from the credit injection. The natural path of the expansion will be transformed into a non-natural excessive economic boom.

5   Sequence of Credit-Driven Booms

Since the inception of active economic policy and modern central banking shortly before and during World War I (Rothbard 1994), natural processes of economic growth rarely occur. Now, economic policy determines the business cycle. The official aims of central banking and government policies are a specific rate of price inflation and low unemployment. Deflation, a general fall of the price fall, even if it is beneficial, must be avoided. This fear of deflation goes so far that central banks define "price level stability" as a positive range of the consumer price index or have begun to call their policy aim as "inflation targeting", which has become the dominant policy model.

The inflationary bias of modern central banks lays the groundwork for the occurrence of the modern boom-and-bust cycles. In the absence of substantial technological progress, modern central banks produce inflation, while in periods of intensive technological progress, they are deceived by low inflation rates. If this is the case, they feel justified expanding the money supply. This way, the central banks themselves have become the originator of credit-driven booms. A policy of inflation targeting entails the tendency to transform a productivity-led economic expansion into a credit-driven economic boom. Productivity gains make it possible that credit expansion comes without price inflation as indicated by the consumer price index. In this framework, and in tune with the fractional reserve banking system, booms, as well as busts, get extended. What would have been only business fluctuations now become big swings. Because monetary expansion is brought about by lower interest rates, businesses will initiate more roundabout production, and consumers as well will ask for more loans. In contrast to a situation where the more roundabout process is being enabled through a resource shift from consumption to higher-order goods as it is given by the trade-off between investment closer and further away from final consumption, a monetary expansion increases overall expenditures, including that for final consumption, while at the same time the falling interest rate calls for an extension of the production process and for more consumption.

The natural path for economic growth is based on productivity which enhances der production possibilities. With a steady money supply, this would lead to falling prices as natural deflation.

Such a non-disruptive, beneficial deflation implies a higher purchasing power. The economy works smoothly and is in stable condition at the higher output and at the lower price level. Such a type of economic expansion occurrs in natural ways when the commodities side expands without an exogenous change of the money supply. Neither the quantity of money nor the cash balances need to change because the changes that occur on the commodities side are in line with the monetary side. In other words, the higher output is matched by a lower price level. If, however, expansionary monetary policy gets applied in pursuit of the policy goal of inflation targeting, the economy is pushed along its cyclical possibilities production frontier into an unsustainable boom. Instead of producing the higher output at a lower price level, inflation targeting produces an additional economic expansion as a boom that comes with a higher price level.

By increasing the money supply, central banks achieve their inflation target, and the economy will get an additional boost, as the additional expansion now comes from the money side. Central bankers and the government celebrate this feat together because apparently the economy is on a perfect path with low rates of inflation and unemployment combined with high rates of economic growth. The monetary authorities feel fully vindicated because high economic growth in a non-inflationary environment has happened. However, this kind of economic expansion is quite different from a movement that would have occurred without central bank intervention. By not letting deflation happen as the natural consequence of productivity gains or other improvements of the factors of production, central banks transform an economic expansion that began on the supply side into a demand-led and credit-driven boom.

Under current central banking policies, such monetary expansions in the face of an ongoing "threatening" deflationary trend may be repeated several times. Each time when the central bank authorities fear deflationary potential, they will be inclined to augment the money supply, thereby pushing the economy to ever higher debt levels. The transformation of the original expansion based on productivity gains into a boom implies that with each intervention the debt levels are brought to higher levels of risk. Neither bankers nor businessmen can opt out even if they possess the insight to understand what is going on. Competition forces the individual business to invest in new capital procedures as soon as they become financially obtainable. In the practical business situation, there is no place for "rational expectations".

There is a stark difference between such a credit-driven boom and a natural economic expansion. While savings together with productivity gains expand the production possibilities in a natural way and allow for a higher purchasing power of money and thus for a higher standard of living, modern active monetary policies, together with the aspirations of government to achieve higher economic growth, overstimulate the economy. Such policies suffer from the illusion that a higher standard of living can be achieved simply by spending more in nominal terms. Things get even worse when governments have accumulated high levels of debt. Then, the authorities will even more abhor deflation because it would increase the debt burden in real terms. For highly indebted governments, inflation, as long as it does not get out of control, becomes attractive. It lowers the debt ratio in real terms and works as an additional tax which remains less visible to the public than the direct increase of taxes. For highly indebted governments, deflation presents a threat.

In the end, scarcity of resources puts a limit on this process and brings about a clash of plans between those economic actors who plan to increase consumption and those that plan to increase investment. As these plans clash, the economy is pushed into a disequilibrium situation where the coordination breaks down. Wages and prices tend to rise accompanied by falling output. The economy moves into a stagflation or worse.

By fighting an apparently dangerous deflation, monetary policy has produced first an unsustainable boom and price inflation later. Should monetary policy now, confronted with visible outbreak of price inflation, switch policies, and initiate a restrictive monetary policy to fight inflation, the higher interest rate would reduce aggregate demand and a recessionary contraction of the economy would occur. If, however, the central bank should continue with expansive monetary policy, the economy would be pushed further forward along the natural production possibilities frontier, and the process of higher demand would also raise the cyclical production possibilities frontier. In this case, the result would be a higher inflation combined with stagnation first, and a recession later. Central bank authorities are confronted with the dilemma of choosing between stagflation now and hyperinflation with an economic collapse later.

Nevertheless, the story does not end here because the exogenously imposed planning error that is put upon the business community entails a massive des-coordination in the economy that in turn provokes a shrinking production capacity. In the longer run it is therefore assured that the natural production possibilities frontier will shrink because of failed business ventures and the loss of confidence. What John Maynard Keynes once blamed on the failing of the "animal spirits" of the business community (Akerlof and Shiller 2010) is in fact the product of governmental policies that have destroyed market coordination and provoked failed businesses and loss of confidence by those that survived the episode. Government policies, with the central bank policy, have brought about malinvestments and disrupted the subtle coordination process of the market process due to false signals about the degrees of feasible roundaboutness and the availability of savings.

The expansion phase has brought about unsustainable production structures that have to be abandoned. Central bank action has transformed the earlier deflationary tendencies into inflationary pressure and then applied measures to curb this tendency to bring about disinflation. By this process, confidence in the business community necessarily will decline. What has happened due to policy intervention has been a structural weakening of the economy's productive capacity. Together with the frustrated state of entrepreneurial spirit, discouraged consumers and the debt load that the expansionary phase had provoked set the stage for the economic depression. By trying to maintain price level stability, monetary policy has brought about destabilization, and by trying to promote economic growth, monetary policy has led to the destruction of the productive capacity.

6   Lessons from the Great Depression

Policymakers claim that laissez-faire capitalism is the culprit of a depression and that an active economic policy is necessary for the economy to recover. This claim, however, neither does hold for the present nor does it explain what happened in the Great Depression (Rothbard 1963). What pushed the US economy into a depression was an active economic policy in the boom years, and what kept the American economy so long in the slump was the active interventionist policy after the bust.

Under the presidency of Herbert Hoover from 1929 to 1933, policy interventionism flourished. Measures designed to prevent a fall in wages hindered the natural course of a rapid economic recovery. Instead of ending the recession, Hoover's interventionism deepened the downturn. President Franklin Delano Roosevelt, who ruled from 1933 until his death in 1945, continued thereafter not only the interventionist policy of Hoover but worsened the policies. Roosevelt practiced ruthless interventionism, which included wage and price controls. He did not hesitate to preach crude anti-capitalism to gain popularity among the masses through cheap and perfidious rhetoric. In the presidential election campaign in 1932, Franklin Delano Roosevelt presented himself as the new Messiah who would save America. Yet he did not know what to do when he took over the presidency in 1933. In practice, his plan comprised pointless hyperactivity. Just doing something was more important to him than doing the right thing. One can only wonder about his policies when one considers with which audacity the government under Roosevelt violated elementary laws of the market.

In order to support the prices of agricultural products, for example, Roosevelt forced the pig farmers to slaughter millions of piglets. To prop up prices for cotton, the farmers had to plow under land. Despite high unemployment, the government prevented lower wage rates. Under Roosevelt's leadership, America came under the spell of a wave of anti-capitalism, and a wild rhetoric damned entrepreneurs and bankers by blaming them for the depression. Roosevelt established a network of informants who monitored prices and wages and spied on the American population. The Great Depression happened not because of the free-market economy, and it lasted so long because of governmental interventions. Not a savage capitalism caused the great crisis, but the duration and depth of the depression resulted from government interventions that first aimed at keeping the boom going beyond its natural cycle in the 1920s and then hampered the recovery with more interventionism after the downturn in the 1930s.

It is not surprising that private investment remained weak under this interventionist onslaught and that the American economy did not emerge from the depression. Until the end of the Roosevelt government in 1945, the American private sector remained in paralysis because of the fear that still more encroachments on property rights were in the making. Only the sectors that profited from war expenditures flourished.

The "Great Depression" was not a failure of capitalism, but the result of World War I, the Treaty of Versailles, and the departure from international free trade. While the tariffs restricted the free movement of goods, the international financial transfers turned into an illusory carousel. The US banks extended loans to the Europeans, particularly to Germany, to pay for the war and reparation debts, which allowed France and the United Kingdom to pay their war debts against the United States.

A fatal blow came with the Smoot-Hawley Tariff Act, which increased tariffs on about 20,000 items. The carousel which got its spin from the lending spree in the 1920s turned into a contracting spiral in the 1930s. When the protectionist measures of the Smoot-Hawley Tariff Act gained legal force on June 17, 1930, the march on the road to the catastrophe speeded up when the world trade collapsed in the following years. As the "Kindleberger-Spiral" chart (Kindleberger 2013) shows, the protectionist measure pushed the world economy into contraction. The monthly decline in world trade from 2998 million to 992 million gold dollars is based on the total world imports from January 1929 to March 1933. When the stock market crashed in October 1929, American money lending ended, and the carousel stopped. The American financial crisis became a global economic contraction.

President Franklin Delano Roosevelt did not lead America out of the depression, but his economic policy measures caused the Great Depression to last so long and run so deep. Unemployment fell only when the US government drafted millions of young men into the military service. The economic expansion in the war years came not from the economy as a productive place but in the form of a war economy, from which consumers did not benefit at all.

In a full assault on capitalism, Roosevelt broke the spirit of the investors and brought down the drive of the entrepreneurs to increase production capacities, accumulate capital, and maintain a well-functioning capital structure.

According to Murray Rothbard's profound analysis of America's Great Depression of 1963, the US government applied a full catalog of false economic policy measures in the 1930s. These interventionist measures explain the depth and length of the economic catastrophe of the Great Depression. Instead of remedying the mistakes that had developed during the boom of the 1920s, the Hoover government, and then Roosevelt, took a whole series of actions that had the opposite effect of correcting the wrong investment and of liberating the forces to readjust the economy.

Roosevelt's economic policy implanted measures that delayed the liquidation of the malinvestments. High wage rates, promoted by the support that the Roosevelt administration gave to the trade unions, led to persistent high unemployment. The American Presidents Hoover and Roosevelt thus exacerbated the errors of the American central bank.

Governments—irrespective of their brand—like to intervene because they love to do things, which other people pay for. Governments like to combat even a small recession because it gives them reasons to launch new spending programs. The financial markets welcome any boosts of liquidity. They call it "stabilization", but it is mainly an arena of political hyperactivism. Yet these policies of stimuli undermine the economy's performance. If the government interferes with the price system by means of maximum and minimum prices, subsidies, and other assistance programs or prohibitions—and, last but not least, by taxation, the interest rate, money supply, and government expenditure policies—government activities distort the original market signals. There will be mistakes in the allocation of resources and the economic competition process will lose its effectiveness. Governments claim to cure the ailment that they themselves are culpable of having brought about.

In the perspective of Austrian macroeconomics, the recession is the phase to cure the excesses of the boom. Therefore, any attempt to postpone the cure deepens the ailment. The best a government can do to promote a swift recovery is to cut taxes and to curtail public spending. Instead of delaying the liquidation of bad investment with the application of "stimulus policies", government policy should be oriented at accelerating the liquidation process. This means that instead of reflating the economy, the central bank should allow deflation to run its course. Likewise, government should refrain from stimulating consumption and instead support more private and public savings. This implies that the public spending should be curtailed.

There are two kinds of deflation. The benign deflation results from productivity gains. It makes the products overall cheaper. If the money supply remains the same, the price level will drop. As a result, the purchasing power grows, and real wages rise. Such beneficial deflation occurs in small steps so that the economic entities can adjust their expectations, and the market interest rate corresponds to the natural rate.

A malignant deflation comes from a collapse of the financial markets. When an abrupt monetary contraction happens, there is no time to adjust the terms of the standing credit relationships. Credit-related defaults will emerge along with imbalances between the amount of old debt and the current market values of the assets. A sudden shrinkage of liquidity, combined with deflation, leads to an unexpected rise in the real interest rate, which makes existing investment projects unprofitable and speeds up the close of new investments.

Austerity policy works when it is combined with free market policies. Austerity need not be painful when the expansion of the private sector accompanies the contraction of the public sector. Igniting the entrepreneurial spirit is the key. The recipe is making the private sector expand while the public sector shrinks.

7   Policy Implications

The "deficits don't matter" school claims that the increase of public debt due to a public deficit would be financed by more tax revenue because government spending "stimulates" the economy. Yet these advocates ignore that the emergence of a debt crisis by itself delivers the evidence that the so-called fiscal multiplier of public expenditure does not work anymore. Those who favor more government expenditures in the face of a public debt crisis suggest that the very same strategy that has led to the calamity would also be its solution.

Recessions and depressions are periods when the imbalances in the economy get corrected in a painful process that is called "forced savings" (Huerta de Soto 2018). It is a period of painful economic contraction because the project that before seemed so profitable has to be abandoned and, in addition to the losses that come with it, there is also the urgent need to build up a new capital structure. The double task is to do away with the old, incorrect capital structure and get the new one. In retrospect, the situation shows that the economy has taken a costly detour and to get back on the right track one must rid of the old track and construct a new one.

It is fundamental for Austrian macroeconomics to consider that economic growth is not only a problem of funding investment but even more so of how to calibrate the size of roundaboutness according to time preference and to choose the appropriate kind of new capital. What is called "technological progress" in modern macroeconomics is necessarily embedded in the entrepreneurial activity. It is intimately linked to the restructuring of the existing capital under the guidance of profitability. Additionally, Austrian macroeconomics includes the caveat that the final judgment about the adequacy of the capital structure is made by the consumers. With the guidance of the routine gone, speculative foresight must come into play to appraise what consumers probably will want in the future and to manage the capital structure accordingly.

That the recession is the consequence of an artificial boom that has brought malinvestment means that the economy has gone too far in a wrong direction. In such a situation, there are few clues available what now is the right track. From the perspective of the entrepreneur, business activity is a continuous exercise of trial and error. This kind of learning process is not confined to the individual firm in an isolated way, but a learning process, in which all firms participate. This means that in a false boom the business community learns the wrong lessons. When the governmental policies no longer work, and the economy falls into a slump, businessmen lose their orientation and are at a loss of knowing with any kind of confidence what to do. The recession shows that something is wrong with the economy, but the fact that during the artificial boom phase the wrong lessons were learned leaves the entrepreneur without knowledge of where the right way would be. It is therefore no wonder when credit demand is weak even if the monetary interest rates are low. Cheap money does not help when the uncertainty looms high about the profitability of investment. Disorientation of the business community in the depression phase leads to caution about new ventures and the interest rate may fall to zero to no avail. The situation is made worse when hyperactive government policy accompanies the perplexity of the business community. Then, the hesitancy to invest will be reinforced by regime uncertainty. "regime uncertainty", as Robert Higgs (1997) has shown, was one of the prime reasons why the Great Depression had continued for so long. Interventionist policies that claim that it takes lower interest rates, new stimuli spending, or other more direct forms of government actions to "grow" the economy again make matters worse. They affect negatively the entrepreneurial search process. The expectation of subsidies may postpone furthermore the beginning of investment activities. Regime uncertainty discourages the inception of the entrepreneurial search process; governmental interventionism blocks the inception of the economic learning process and thus blocks economic progress. The more the government becomes irrationally hyperactive, the more business will recede and the longer will it take for the upswing to come.

Different from conventional macroeconomic modeling, Austrian macroeconomics has always held fast to the rule that macroeconomic phenomena must be linked to their microeconomic basis. Likewise different from mainstream macroeconomics is the caveat of Austrian economics that the distinction between the short and the long run is artificial. The long run is nothing but the result of a series of short-term events. The link between micro and macro and between the short and the long run is capital. Opening the black box of conventional macroeconomics and introducing the stages of production, Austrian macroeconomics opens the view to a wide spectrum of economic policy issues. The lack of authentic savings as a source of investment shows up as the consequence of money creation by the central bank and a financial system that is based on fractional reserves. Institutional arrangements of this kind and a policy orientation toward a set of macroeconomic goals are inherently prone to bring about production structures that are unsustainable which later must be abandoned at high cost. Another important aspect which Austrian macroeconomics highlights is that economic policies can be deeply flawed even when such indicators as the price index and the data for economic growth suggest that the economy is on the path of stable expansion.

Capitalist production takes place as roundaboutness and results in higher productivity, thereby providing increased levels of consumable output. Roundabout production is time consuming and requires that for some time consumption or potential consumption is given up in favor of a restructuring of the production process and the shifting of investment away from immediate consumption toward the higher stages of production. Roundabout production brings with it an economic expansion that lifts the natural production possibilities and, ceteris paribus, results in a lower price level. This natural deflation implies a higher purchasing power, and the productivity increase brings down the cyclical production possibilities frontier to the level of higher productivity in terms of costs. As a result, the economy works at a higher output with a lower price level. The economic expansion has occurred in a natural way through the application of roundaboutness based on foregone consumption without exogenous changes in money. Neither the monetary aggregate nor its velocity needs change as the relevant changes occur in compensatory form when the higher production is matched by lower prices.

Under the current institutional arrangements of active central banking, however, that is oriented toward macroeconomic policy goals and a monetary regime based on fractional reserve banking, there is no cure for the perpetual occurrence of extreme business cycles. It is the unavoidable outcome of these institutional arrangements that unsustainable production structures will be brought about that bring with them distortions and tensions within the economy, particularly between the resources made available through savings and the investment that takes place.

The policy implications of Austrian macroeconomics are quite different from the conventional economics. In the perspective of Austrian Economics, the recipe against the boom-bust cycle is to refrain from instigating the boom. It is not to expect, however, that central banks would accept deflation at a stage in the sequence of the business cycle when it is possible to fabricate a boom with only moderate inflation rates. Therefore, the more general conclusion of Austrian macroeconomics for the conduct of monetary policy says that instead of pursuing the futile endeavor to improve central bank management, one should search for solutions that will transform the monetary system into a decentralized system that is not subject to active central banking. Options range from the "Bitcoin Standard" to free banking or a modern gold standard (White 2023).

Austrian macroeconomics is a theory about avoiding deep recessions and depressions. It is not to be misunderstood as a magic tool to get the economy out of the slump. The cure for slump is to prevent it, which means, most of all, the absence of governmental interventions and the avoidance of irritating policy regime changes. It usually takes time until the natural impulse of human beings to improve their economic position will reawaken and the "animal spirits" will return to the business community. The other lesson in Austrian macroeconomics is that the prime cure for the boom-bust cycle is the prevention of the artificial boom. As the general conclusion for monetary policy, the lesson says that instead of pursuing the futile endeavor to improve central bank management, one should search for institutional solutions that make the monetary system more autonomous beyond the need for active central banking.

As Ludwig von Mises (1952) adverted, "(a)ll that a good government can do to improve the well-being of the masses is the establishment and preservation of the institutional frameworks that do not hinder the accumulation of new capital and its use to improve the technical production methods." Trouble starts when governments instigate an artificial boom and sometimes even worse when they try to keep the false boom going on.

Under the condition of productivity gains due to technological progress, monetary policy oriented at price stability is prone to provoke an unsustainable boom. Instead of allowing deflation to run its course, monetary authorities pursue so-called stabilization policies. This way, they push the economy on a path to debt accumulation. The more intensive the technological advances and the cost reductions will be, and the longer the period will continue when monetary policy holds down the interest rate, the more the economy will be induced to increase its debt levels. The size of the debt level relative to the productive base at the peak of the boom will make monetary policy ineffective once the contraction phase starts.

In the case of a dearth of productivity gains and under the condition of rising labor costs, the monetary inflationary bias of modern central banks produces price inflation and stagflation, as expansive monetary policy feeds directly into higher consumer prices. It is mainly under the conditions of high productivity gains or when other factors bring down production costs on a large scale—for example, due to the global extension of the division of labor—that central banks have an easy shot at achieving "price-level stability" and of keeping the price inflation rate within their established target. This way, however, central banks are misled about the consequence of monetary expansion, as it does not yet show up right away in the consumer price index. Because modern macroeconomics fully ignores the impact of the interest rate on the capital structure, most monetary policy authorities are unaware that an economic expansion that began on the supply side may easily turn it into a demand-driven unsustainable boom based on credit creation due to their own ingenuous monetary policy.

All credit expansion must come to an end at some point in time. The more debt has been accumulated, the more vulnerable the structure becomes so that even otherwise minor shocks can topple the inverted pyramid. Small causes may have big effects. This is why the turning point comes so often as a surprise. Suddenly, and apparently without obvious reason, so it seems, the foundation on which the upside down pyramid of debt was erected begins to erode. Debt-free economic growth could have been achieved if the central bank had let a short-lived deflationary episode happen. Yet instead, guided by the rule of targeting the price level, the monetary authorities tend to fight any signs of price deflation. Thus, by following the policy rule of "price stability" they inadvertently create a credit-driven excessive boom. At the first stage of the monetary expansion, interest rate policy produces an economic upswing; at the peak of the boom, the debt load has made the economy vulnerable even to otherwise harmless adversities. Shocks that would hardly affect a robust economy now represent a threat. Central bank management becomes increasingly precarious, and the tendency increases to fight as hard as possible against any potential downturn with further increases in the money supply.

In terms of the capital structure of the economy (Hayek 1931; Garrison 2001, 2005), both the goods nearer to consumption and those nearer to the investment side with larger time horizons get the main incentives from monetary expansion. For the consumer, consumption goods become more easily attainable, while for businesses, the acquisition of better capital goods that render higher productivity can be financed more easily. In contrast to a constellation when authentic savings increase because cash holders reduce their potential consumption and provide funds for investment and/or consumption by the credit takers, a purely monetary expansion creates the illusion that more savings appear to be available than there are in terms of the de facto availability of resources as it is given by the production possibilities. Thus, demand for investment goods (particularly at the early stages of the production process) will increase along with the demand for consumer goods.

In order to allow an expansion of the monetary base, central banks must lower their interest rate, which, in the case of the United States, is the Federal Funds Rate. This interest rate serves only as an anchor for the interest rates for the longer term. In fact, it is an anchor with a very elastic chain. Here, too, we confront the phenomenon that when the storm comes up, the elasticity of the chain rises: Often beyond the imagination of the model-makers whose expectations are formed by the working of the model under smooth conditions.

At the end of the boom phase, productivity gains will peter out or adverse supply side shocks will occur that no longer can be easily absorbed. With the absence of compensating productivity gains, monetary impulses now feed directly into commodity prices. When central banks continue with monetary expansion, price inflation will result. With inflation rising, the monetary multiplier and the velocity of circulation tend to increase and drive furthermore the price level upward. Without drastic changes, the economy moves on the path to hyperinflation.

In the case of a natural growth process, consumption would be below its full potential as it is given by current production so that funds can be obtained to sustain investment. The waiting time until maturity of the investment project reflects the current state of time preference. In a credit-driven boom, the link between authentic savings and the time it takes to finish an investment project is artificially severed, and when the interest rate is set too low, illusions about available funding will be produced. In the modern macroeconomic accounting framework, the creation of imbalances will count as "economic growth" although it is fake growth even though employment may rise. It is only at the turning point from boom to bust when the imbalances become visible and when unemployment increases. In order to correct the imbalances that have been built up due to overspending, forced savings in order to rebalance the economy characterize the bust.

One can simplify the notion of the capital structure by assuming only three stages with the end phase leading to the final product and to the point of consumption. In an artificial boom, both the first part and the last part of the structure get a boost. Given that the artificiality of the boom consists in the fact of insufficient supply of funds, it will be the middle part that must give in. Research and development as part of the earliest stages of production get a boost along with final consumption goods. The middle part, mainly industrial production, recedes. In the case of the US economy that phenomenon could be observed by the transformation of its production structure when the loss of production in the middle part had to be compensated by the import of tradeable goods.

Beginning with the assumption of a well-coordinated economy in which the various stages of production, guided by the natural rate of interest, interact smoothly according to the prevailing time preference, a change in the political rate of interest disrupts the economic coordination. When the central bank lowers the interest below its natural level, it produces a signal that says that more funding is available even if this is not the case. Given that the time preferences of the economic actors have not changed, the lower interest rate will tend to induce a reduction of authentic saving and implicitly lead to a rise in consumption while, at the same time, business investment will also act following the same signal and increase investment. The stages nearer and those further away to final consumption will experience an increase in investment, while the middle part of the production stream comes under pressure. Yet given that the time preference has not changed and therefore no additional authentic saving is available, this expansion of stage one and stage three comes at the cost of stage two. In stage two, disinvestment will happen to finance the expansion of stage one and stage three. In practice, it is enough that stage two receives no new investment as then depreciation will cause a shrinking of this stage. The result is an unsustainable production structure characterized by the disrupted coordination which was brought about by the atrophy of the middle stage, which has led to the overextension of the earlier and later stages of production. Rebuilding the new capital structure is a difficult and tedious process during which businesses are at high risk to fail because the economy cannot simply return to the former production structure but must discover its new form. In other words, what has happened here is a loss of resources and a loss of time, resources and time that in the absence of a wrong interest rate policy could have been used to discover and build the new coordination pattern over time instead of following the wrong path which involves sunken costs and the loss of time. The policy of monetary stimulus has not led to an increase in economic wealth but has reduced the economy's production possibilities. The empirical evidence of this process shows up as stagnating productivity gains. Sustainable expansion would have required a shift of resources from consumption to roundabout investment.

As its conclusion, Austrian macroeconomics states that sustainable economic booms are characterized by high productivity gains due to new technology and are often accompanied by an increase in the supply of labor. This combination should lead to benevolent deflation. Yet by not allowing that this benevolent deflation would run its course, central banks boost the natural boom to excessive dimensions. This happens even when they meet their inflation target. They provide ample liquidity in a situation where deflation would be required. The expansion of the money supply beyond authentic savings comes along with increasing debt levels. In such a situation, manufactured by central banks, when an excessive debt level relative to the productive base has been reached, deflation indeed becomes a problem. In a low-debt economy, the positive effects of deflation in terms of increased purchasing power outweigh its negative side and will be beneficial. In a high-debt economy, deflation becomes vicious. Therefore, modern central banks will be inclined to make the debt surge go on as far and as long as they can.

REFERENCES

Akerlof and Shiller (2010): George A. Akerlof and Robert J. Shiller. Animal Spirits: How Human Psychology Drives the Economy, and Why It Matters for Global Capitalism. Princeton University Press.

Bagus, Philipp (2020): The Quality of Money. QJAE. *Quarterly Journal of Austrian Economics* 12, no. 4: 22–45. https://mises.org/quarterly-journal-austrian-economics/quality-money-0

Barro, Robert (1989). "New Classicals and Keynesians, or the Good Guys and the Bad Guys". *NBER Working Paper* No. 2982. May 1989.

Baumol and Blinder (1997): William J. Baumol and Alan A. Blinder. Economics: Principles and Policy. Cengage Learning.

Bernanke, Ben S. et al. (2001). Inflation targeting: Lessons from the international experience. Princeton Univ. Press. 2001. https://www.amazon.com/-/pt/dp/0691086893

Bernanke and Mishkin (1997). Ben S. Bernanke and Frederic S. Mishkin. Inflation Targeting: A New Framework for Monetary Policy? Journal of Economic Perspectives. vol. 11, no. 2, Spring 1997 (pp. 97–116) https://www.aeaweb.org/articles?id=10.1257/jep.11.2.97

Blanchard (2008): Olivier Blanchard: The State of Macro. NBER. National Bureau of Economic Research. August 2008. https://www.nber.org/papers/w14259

Blanchard et al. (2010). Olivier Blanchard, Giovanni Dell'Ariccia, and Paulo Mauro. Rethinking Macroeconomic Policy. *IMF Staff Position Note.* January 2010. https://www.imf.org/external/pubs/ft/spn/2010/spn1003.PDF

© The Author(s), under exclusive license to Springer Nature
Switzerland AG 2024
A. P. Mueller, *A Primer on Austrian Macroeconomics,*
Palgrave Studies in Austrian Economics,
https://doi.org/10.1007/978-3-031-75189-9

Blinder (1999). Alan S. Blinder. Central Banking in Theory and Practice (Lionel Robbins Lectures) MIT Press.

Buchanan (1969): James M. Buchanan, Is Economics the Science of Choice? in: Roads to Freedom. Essays in Honor of Friedrich A. von Hayek, ed. By Erich Streissler et al., London 1969, pp. 47–64.

Buiter (2009): Willem Buiter. The unfortunate uselessness of most 'state of the art' academic monetary economics. *Financial Times*. March 3, 2009. http:// blogs.ft.com/maverecon/2009/03/the-unfortunate-uselessness-of-most-state-of-the-art-academic-monetary-economics/#axzz2scEBA7bn

Boettke (1994) Peter J. Boettke: *The Elgar Companion to Austrian Economics*. Cheltenham, UK: Edward Elgar Publishing Limited.

Böhm-Bawerk (1884): Eugen von Böhm-Bawerk. *Kapital und Kapitalzins*. Innsbruck: Wagner (English translation: Capital and Interest: A Critical History of Economical Theory. London: Macmillan and Co. 1890.

Böhm-Bawerk (1884): Eugen von Böhm-Bawerk. The Positive Theory of Capital. London Macmillan (The Positive Theory of Capital, 1891) https://oll.liberty-fund.org/titles/smart-the-positive-theory-of-capital

Böhm-Bawerk (1890): Eugen von Böhm-Bawerk. Capital and Interest: A Critical History of Economic Theory. London Macmillan. https://oll.libertyfund.org/titles/smart-capital-and-interest-a-critical-history-of-economic-theory

Bradford (2000). The Triumph of Monetarism? *Journal of Economic Perspectives*. Vol. 14, No. 1 (Winter) 2000, pp. 83–94. https://www.aeaweb.org/articles?id=10.1257/jep.14.1.83

Braun (2024). Braun, Eduard. Capital is not a factor of production but organizes the allocation and distribution of resources in capitalism. The Review of Austrian Economics. https://link.springer.com/article/10.1007/s11138-024-00655-1

Cachanosky, N. and Salter, A.W. The view from Vienna: An analysis of the renewed interest in the Mises-Hayek theory of the business cycle. *Review of Austrian Economics* (2017) 30: 169. https://doi.org/10.1007/s11138-016-0340-5

Coase, Ronald (2012). "Saving Economics from the Economists". *Harvard Business Review*. December 2012.

Cochran (1998) John P. Cochran. The Role of Fractional-Reserve Banking and Financial Intermediation in the Money Supply Process: Keynes and the Austrians. *Quarterly Journal of Austrian Economics*. Vol. 1. No. 3 (Fall 1998): 29–40. https://mises.org/quarterly-journal-austrian-economics/role-fractional-reserve-banking-and-financial-intermediation-money-supply-process-keynes-and-austrians

Cochrane (2023) John H. Cochrane. The Fiscal Theory of the Price Level. Princeton University Press.

Cochrane et al. (2020): John Cochrane and John B. Taylor. Strategies for Monetary Policy. Hoover Institution Press.

Cochrane (2013): John H. Cochrane. "The New-Keynesian Liquidity Trap". *University of Chicago Booth School of Business. Research Paper.* September 2013. http://faculty.chicagobooth.edu/john.cochrane/research/papers/zero_bound_2.pdf

Colander, David (1995). "The Stories We Tell. A Reconsideration of AS/AD Analysis". Journal of Economic Perspectives. Volume 9, Number 3. Summer 1995. pp. 169–188. https://www.aeaweb.org/articles?id=10.1257/jep.9.3.169

Copernicus, Nicolaus (1526): Monetae cudendae ratio. Memorandum to Prussian Diet. Available at: https://la.wikisource.org/wiki/Monetae_cudendae_ratio

Cwik (2024) Austrian Business Cycle Theory: An Introduction. The Ludwig von Mises Institute. Auburn, Ala. https://mises.org/library/book/austrian-business-cycle-theory-introduction

Ebeling (1991) Richard M. Ebeling (ed.): Austrian Economics. A Reader, Hillsdale, Michigan 1991 (Hillsdale College Press).

Faust, Jon (2012). DSGE Models: I Smell a Rat (and It Smells Good). *International Journal of Central Banking.* March 2012, pp. 53–64.

Federal Reserve Bank of Dallas (2021): Enrique Martínez-García, Jarod Coulter and Valerie Grossman. Fed's new inflation targeting policy seeks to maintain well-anchored inflation expectations. Federal Reserve Bank of Dallas. April 6, 2021. https://www.dallasfed.org/research/economics/2021/0406

Fisher, Irving, with Harry G. Brown (1911). *The Purchasing Power of Money.* New York: Macmillan. Reprinted in *The Works of Irving Fisher*, (Fisher 1997), Vol. 4.

Fisher, Irving (1933). The Debt-Deflation Theory of the Great Depression. *Econometrica.* Vol. 1, No. 4 (Oct. 1933), pp. 337–357.

Foltyn, Richard (2014). Dynamics in the Solow-Swan Growth Model. Wolfram Demonstrations Project. Available at: http://demonstrations.wolfram.com/DynamicsInTheSolowSwanGrowthModel/

Friedman, Milton (1956) *The quantity theory of money—A restatement*, in Friedman M. (ed.) Studies in the Quantity Theory of Money, Chicago, University of Chicago Press.

Friedman (1961) Milton Friedman: The Lag in Effect of Monetary Policy. Journal of Political Economy. Vol. 69, No. 5 (Oct., 1961), pp. 447–466.

Galbács, Peter (2015). *The Theory of New Classical Macroeconomics. A Positive Critique.* Heidelberg/New York/Dordrecht/London: Springer.

Garrison, Roger (2001). *Time and Money. The Macroeconomics of Capital Structure.* London and New York: Routledge Foundation of the Market Economy 2001.

Garrison (2005): Roger Garrison. The Austrian School: Capital-Based Macroeconomics. Chapter 9 in *Modern Macroeconomics: Its Origins, Development and Current State,* edited by Brian Snowdon and Howard

R. Vane. Aldershot: Edward Elgar, 2005 https://webhome.auburn. edu/~garriro/cbm.pdf

Gordon, Robert J. (2013). The Phillips Curve is Alive and Well: Inflation and the NAIRU During the Slow Recovery. *NBER Working Paper* No. 19390. August 2013. https://www.nber.org/papers/w19390

Handbook of Economic Expectations (2023). Edited by Ruediger Bachmann, Giorgio Topa, Wilbert van der Klaauw. Academic Press https://www.amazon. com/-/pt/dp/0128229276

Hayek (1931): Friedrich A. v. Hayek. Prices and Production and Other Works. Ludwig von Mises Institute 2008. https://cdn.mises.org/prices_and_production_and_other_works.pdf

Hayek (1935): F. A. Hayek (ed.), Collectivist Economics Planning: Critical Studies on the Possibilities of Socialism, London 1935.

Hayek (1941): Friedrich A. v. Hayek. The Pure Theory of Capital. Ludwig von Mises Institute. https://mises.org/library/book/pure-theory-capital

Hayek (1969). F.A. v. Hayek, Der Wettbewerb als Entdeckungsverfahren, in: Freiburger Studien, Tübingen 1969.

Hayek (1974): Friedrich Hayek. The Pretence of Knowledge. (Nobel Prize Lecture 1974) https://www.nobelprize.org/prizes/economic-sciences/1974/hayek/lecture/

Hayek (1979): Friedrich A. v. Hayek. Scientism and the Study of Society, in: The Counter-Revolution of Science (Indianapolis: Liberty Press, 1979).

Hayek (1984): Friedrich A. v. Hayek. Intertemporal Price Equilibrium and Movement in the Value of Money, in: *Money, Capital and Fluctuations. Early Essays*. Chicago: The University of Chicago Press, pp. 71–117.

Hayek (1995): Friedrich August von Hayek, The Economics of the 1930s as seen from London, in: The Collected Works of F. A. Hayek, Vol. 9, Contra Keynes and Cambridge, ed. by Bruce Caldwell, London 1995 (University of Chicago Press).

Hennings (1997): The Austrian Theory of Value and Capital. Studies in the Life and Work of Eugen von Böhm-Bawerk. Cheltenham and Brookfield: Edward Elgar.

Herbener (2011). Jeffrey M. Herbener. *Pure Time-Preference Theory of Interest*. Ludwig von Mises Institute. Auburn, Ala. 2011, edited by Jeffrey M. Herbener. https://cdn.mises.org/The%20Pure%20Time-Preference%20Theory%20of%20Interest_2.pdf

Herbener (2002): Jeffrey M. Herbener. Herbener, J. M. (2002): After the Age of Inflation. Austrian Proposals for Monetary Reform. Quarterly Journal of Austrian Economics. Vol. 5. No. 4 (Winter 2002): 5–19.

Hicks, John (1937). Mr. Keynes and the 'Classics'. A Suggested Interpretation. *Econometrica*. Vol. 5, No. 2, April 1937, pp. 147–159.

Hicks, John (1980/81). IS-LM: An Explanation. *Journal of Post-Keynesian Economics.* Vol. III, No. 2, pp. 139–154.

Higgs (1997): Robert Higgs: Regime Uncertainty: Why the Great Depression Lasted So Long and Why Prosperity Resumed after the War. The Independent Review Vol. 1, No. 4 (Spring 1997), pp. 561–590.

Howden, David: The Quantity Theory of Money. *Journal of Prices & Markets* (2013) 1.1: 17–30. https://core.ac.uk/download/pdf/213996976.pdf

Huerta de Soto, Jesús (2012). Jesús Huerta de Soto. *Money, Bank Credit, and Economic Cycles.* 3rd edition. Auburn, Ala.: The Ludwig von Mises Institute. https://mises.org/library/book/money-bank-credit-and-economic-cycles

Huerta de Soto (2018) Jesús Huerta de Soto. Artificial Booms and Forced Savings. Mises Wire. https://mises.org/mises-wire/artificial-booms-and-theory-forced-saving

Holcombe (1999): Randall G. Holcombe (ed.), Fifteen Great Austrian economists. The Mises Institute 1999.

Holcombe, R. G. (2003): Progress and Entrepreneurship. *Quarterly Journal of Austrian Economics.* Vol. 6. No. 3 (Fall 2003): 3–26.

Hume, David (1752). *Of Money,* in Essays. London: George Routledge and Sons.

Hülsmann (1998): Jörg Guido Hülsmann. Toward a General Theory of Error Cycles. Quarterly Journal of Austrian Economics. Volume 1, No. 4 (Winter 1998) https://cdn.mises.org/qjae1_4_1.pdf

Keynes, John M. (1924). *A Tract on Monetary Reform.* London: Macmillan.

Keynes, John M. (1936). The General Theory of Employment, Interest, and Money. London: Macmillan.

King (2002): J. E. King. A History of Post Keynesian Economics Since 1936. Edward Elgar Publishing.

Kindleberger (2013): Charles P. Kindleberger. The World in Depression, 1929–1939. University of California Press.

Koenig, Evan F. (2012). All in the Family: The Close Connection Between Nominal-GDP Targeting and the Taylor Rule. *Staff Papers of the Federal Reserve Bank of Dallas* No. 17, March 2012.

Kirzner (1985): Israel M. Kirzner. Discovery and the Capitalist Process. University of Chicago Press.

Kirzner (1972): Israel M. Kirzner. Competition and Entrepreneurship, in: The Collected Works of Israel M. Kirzner, ed. By Peter J. Boettke 2013.

Kirzner (1973). Israel M. Kirzner. Competition and Entrepreneurship. University of Chicago Press 1973

Klein (1992): Peter G. Klein (ed.) The Fortunes of Liberalism, Vol. 4, The Collected Works of F.A. Hayek. Chicago and London 1992.

Kregel J.A. (1985). Hamlet without the Prince: Cambridge Macroeconomics without Money. *The American Economic Review.* Vol. 75. No.2. Papers and Proceedings of the Ninety-Seventh Annual Meeting of the American Economic Association (May 1985), pp. 133–139.

Lachmann (1956): Ludwig Lachmann. Capital and its Structure. The Ludwig von Mises Institute. https://mises.org/library/book/capital-and-its-structure

Lachmann. (1977). Ludwig Lachman. Capital, Expectations, and the Market Process. Ludwig von Mises Institute, Auburn, Ala 1974. https://mises.org/library/book/capital-expectations-and-market-process

Lachmann (1991): Ludwig M. Lachmann: The Market Economy and the Distribution of Wealth, in: Richard M. Ebeling (ed.): Austrian Economics. A Reader, Hillsdale, Michigan 1991 (Hillsdale College Press), pp. 670–686.

Laidler, David (2013). Three Revolutions in Macroeconomics: their Nature and Influence. Economic Policy Research Institute. *EPRI Working Paper Series.* University of Western Ontario. London, Ontario. http://economics.uwo.ca/epri/workingpapers_docs/wp2013/Laidler_04.pdf

Lewin, Peter (1998). Capital in Disequilibrium: The Role of Capital in a Changing World (Routledge Foundations of the Market Economy). Routledge. 1998.

Lewin et al (2019). Peter Lewin. Austrian Capital Theory: A Modern Survey of the Essentials (Elements in Austrian Economics). Cambridge University Press.

Lewin (2021): Peter Lewin and Nicolás Cachanosky. Capital and Finance. Theory and History. Routledge.

Mankiw, Gregory N. (2006). The Macroeconomist as Scientist and Engineer. *Journal of Economic Perspectives.* Volume 20, Number 4, Fall 2006, pp. 29–46. https://www.aeaweb.org/articles?id=10.1257/jep.20.4.29

Mankiw and Reis (2010). N. Gregory Mankiw and Ricardo Reis. Imperfect Information and Aggregate Supply. Chapter 5. Handbook of Monetary Economics. Vol. 3. https://econpapers.repec.org/bookchap/eeemonhes/3.htm

McCraw (2009). Thomas K. McCraw. Prophet of Innovation: Joseph Schumpeter and Creative Destruction. Belknap Press.

Mises (1912). Ludwig von Mises. *Theorie des Geldes und der Umlaufsmittel. München.* Duncker & Humblot (English version: The Theory of Money and Credit. Indianapolis: Liberty Fund 1980).

Mises, Ludwig von (1952): Planning for Freedom. Libertarian Press.

Mises, Ludwig von (1989). *Human Action. A Treatise on Economics.* The Scholar's Edition. Auburn, Ala.: The Ludwig von Mises Institute.

Menger (1871) Carl Menger. Grundsätze der Volkswirthschaftslehre. https://oll.libertyfund.org/titles/menger-grundsatze-der-volkswirtschaftslehre. Principles of Economics. https://mises.org/library/book/principles-economics

Menger (1892): Carl Menger. "Geld". Collected Works Vol. IV. https://cdn.mises.org/Collected%20Works%20of%20Carl%20Menger%20%28in%20German%29%20Volume%20IV_5.pdf

Mundell (2000) Robert A Mundell. A Reconsideration of the Twentieth Century. American Economic Review. vol. 90, no. 3, June 2000 (pp. 327–340). https://www.aeaweb.org/articles?id=10.1257/aer.90.3.327

Mishkin, Frederic S. (1991). Is the Fisher Effect for Real? A Reexamination of the Relationship Between Inflation and Interest Rates. *NBER Working Paper.* No. 3632 May 1993.

Mueller (2018): Antony P. Mueller. Capital and the Business Cycle – A Synthesis with a didactic exposition. (SSRN March 15, 2018). https://doi.org/10.2139/ssrn.3141447

Mueller (2021). Where Prices Come From. Mises Wire. https://mises.org/miseswire/where-prices-come-menger-explains

O'Driscoll et al. (1985): Gerald P. O'Driscoll, G and Mario Rizzo. The Economics of Time and Ignorance. Routledge Foundations of the Market Economy.

Phelps, Edmund (1967). "Phillips curves, expectations and optimal unemployment over time". *Economica, New Series,* 34930, pp. 254–281.

Phelps, Edmund (1968). "Money Wage Dynamics and Labor Market Equilibrium." *Journal of Political Economy.* July/August, 76:4, pt. 2, pp. 678–711.

Romer, David (2000). Keynesian Macroeconomics without the LM curve. *Journal of Economic Perspectives.* Vol. 14, No. 2 (Spring), pp. 149–169.

Rothbard (1962): Murray N. Rothbard, Man, Economy, and State. A Treatise on Economic Principles, Auburn, Ala. 2001 (The Ludwig von Mises Institute), first published in 1962.

Rothbard (1963): Murray N. Rothbard. America's Great Depression. The Ludwig von Mises Institute. https://mises.org/library/book/americas-great-depression

Rothbard. (1994). Murray N. Rothbard: The Case Against the FED. Ludwig von Mises Institute, Auburn, Ala. 1994. https://mises.org/library/book/case-against-fed

Rothbard (2006): Murray Rothbard, The Mantle of Science, Mises Daily, March 11, 2006).

Rowley (2004): Charles K Rowley and Friedrich Schneider, eds. *The Encyclopedia of Public Choice.* 2 vols. Boston: Kluwer, 2004.

Salerno (2007): Joseph T. Salerno. What is Causal-Realist Approach? Mises Wire. https://mises.org/mises-daily/whata-causal-realist-approch

Salerno (2012): Joseph T. Salerno. A Reformulation of Austrian Business Cycle Theory in Light of the Financial Crisis. *Quarterly Journal of Austrian Economics.* Vol. 15, No. 1 (Spring), pp. 3–44.

Selgin, G. (1994): Free Banking and Monetary Control. *Economic Journal.* Vol. 104, No. 427, pp. 1449–1459.

Shackle (1949): Probability and Uncertainty. Macroeconomica. Vol. 1, Issue 3, October 1949, pp. 161–173. https://onlinelibrary.wiley.com/doi/10.1111/j.1467-999X.1949.tb00040.x

Sen, Amartya: On Some Debates in Capital Theory Author(s): *Economica, New Series,* Vol. 41, No. 163 (August 1974), pp. 328–335.

Strigl (2000): Richard von Strigl. Capital and Production. The Mises Institute. https://mises.org/library/book/capital-and-production

Taylor, John B. (1999). A Historical Analysis of Monetary Policy Rules. In: *Monetary Policy Rules*. Chicago. University of Chicago Press, pp. 319–47.

Taylor (1997) John B. Taylor. The Policy Rule Mix: A Macroeconomic policy Evaluation. Stanford University. https://web.stanford.edu/~johntayl/Onlinepaperscombinedbyyear/2000/2000/The_Policy_Rule_Mix_A_Macroeconomic_Policy_Evaluation.pdf

Thornton, Daniel L. (2013). Is Nominal GDP Targeting a Rule Policymakers Could Accept? Federal Reserve Bank of St. Louis. Economic Synopses, 2013, No. 29.

Wicksell (1898): Knut Wicksell. Geldzins und Güterpreise: Eine Studie über die den Tauschwert des Geldes bestimmenden Ursachen. Jena, 1898. (Interest and Prices. The Ludwig von Mises Institute) https://mises.org/library/book/interest-and-prices

White (1993). Lawrence H. White (ed.). Free Banking. Cheltenham. Edward Elgar.

White (2023). Lawrence H. White. Better Money. Cambridge University Press.

HANDBOOK OF MONETARY ECONOMICS

Martínez-Garcia et al.: Fed's new inflation targeting policy seeks to maintain well-anchored inflation expectations. Federal Reserve Bank.of Dallas. April 06, 2021 https://www.dallasfed.org/research/economics/2021/0406

Mueller (2020). The Magic Money Tree. The Case Against Moden Monetary Theory. Research Paper Series of the Adam Smith Institute (ASI), London. Also available at Social Science Research Network (SSRN). https://papers.ssrn.com/sol3/papers.cfm?abstract_id=3641683

Rothbard (1999).The Origin of the Federal Reserve. The Quarterly Journal of Austrian Economics. Vol. 2, No. 3 (Fall 1999). https://cdn.mises.org/qjae2_3_1.pdf

Salerno (2010). Joseph T. Salerno. Money: Sound and Unsound. Ludwig von Mises Institute 2010

INDEX

© The Author(s), under exclusive license to Springer Nature
Switzerland AG 2024
A. P. Mueller, *A Primer on Austrian Macroeconomics*,
Palgrave Studies in Austrian Economics,
https://doi.org/10.1007/978-3-031-75189-9

The manufacturer's authorised representative in the EU is Springer
Nature Customer Service Centre GmbH, Europaplatz 3, 69115 Heidelberg,
Germany. If you have any concerns regarding our products, please
contact ProductSafety@springernature.com

Printed and bound by CPI Group (UK) Ltd, Croydon, CR0 4YY

29/04/2026

02099538-0005